Churches for Communities

St John the Baptist, Stadhampton.
An arch created by new stackable chairs, September 2013.
PHOTO MIKE PECKETT

BECKY PAYNE

CHURCHES FOR COMMUNITIES

ADAPTING OXFORDSHIRE'S CHURCHES FOR WIDER USE

OXFORDSHIRE HISTORIC CHURCHES TRUST

First published in Great Britain 2014
by the Oxfordshire Historic Churches Trust
c/o The Hon. Secretary
Jonathan Scheele, 20 Portland Road, Oxford, OX2 7EY

British Library Cataloguing in Publication Data
A catalogue record for this book is available from the British Library

ISBN 978 0 9927693 0 7

Edited by Elisabeth Ingles
Designed by Lucy or Robert
Printed and bound in Great Britain by
Berforts Information Press, Eynsham, Oxford

Front cover St John the Baptist, Burford.
Chairs facing north to hear students from the Ssese Islands
on exchange with Burford School singing at a Sunday service, July 2008.
PHOTO ST JOHN THE BAPTIST CHURCH, BURFORD

Back cover St Peter and St Paul, Deddington,
the Farmers' Market, July 2013.
PHOTO JUDY WARD

CONTENTS

BANBURY ●

St Peter,
Hook Norton

St Peter and St Paul,
Deddington

CHIPPING NORTON ●

M40

St Mary and St Edburga, Stratton Audley

St Nicholas,
Chadlington

St Edburg, Bicester

St Nicholas, Tackley

St Mary the Virgin,
Charlbury

St Mary the Virgin,
Kirtlington

St John the Baptist,
Burford

St Thomas of Canterbury,
Elsfield

St Mary the Virgin, Witney

St Michael at the North Gate, Oxford

New Road Baptist Church, Oxford

OXFORD

St Mary the Virgin, Thame

St Luke, Oxford

St Peter and St Paul,
Aston Rowant

St John the Baptist,
Stadhampton

Trinity Church, Abingdon

St Helen, Abingdon

St Mary the Virgin,
Chalgrove

St John the Evangelist,
Fernham

DIDCOT ●

St Agatha, Brightwell-cum-Sotwell

St Mary le More, Wallingford

St John the Evangelist, Stoke Row

St Thomas of Canterbury,
Goring-on-Thames

10 mi

20 km

PREFACE

The Oxfordshire Historic Churches Trust was founded fifty years ago to provide financial help for repairs and practical enhancements for historic places of worship of all denominations in Oxfordshire; to encourage wider interest in them; and to raise funds to enable us to do this. Our vision is that in fifty years' time Oxfordshire's historic churches will still be fit for their threefold purpose – for worship, as a heritage valued by society and as a community resource. We believe that this is all the more vital because these buildings provide links to our past – and we live in such a rapidly changing world.

We accept that it will become increasingly important for the survival of these buildings that they should be used for other purposes as well as for worship. Within our limited means we are therefore happy to support projects for practical enhancements designed to make this possible.

We are delighted to publish this collection of studies showing how some of Oxfordshire's churches have responded to the challenge. Every case is different, and our aim is not to provide models that other churches and the communities around them should follow slavishly but a series of examples – some of which may perhaps seem more successful than others – that they can use when they are discussing what solution would be right for their particular circumstances.

We see this volume therefore not just as a celebration of what has been done but as a stimulus and tool for those who may be considering such projects in the future. It is also a very appropriate way for us to mark our fiftieth birthday and thus the start of our second fifty years of helping Oxfordshire's churches.

We are very grateful to Becky Payne for all her painstaking work, to Bishop Colin whose concept it was and to all those others who have contributed to this project.

Basil Eastwood, CMG
Chairman, Oxfordshire Historic Churches Trust
November 2013

St Luke, Oxford.
St Luke's Triptych, which features members of the church and local
community, was painted by the Revd Jane Sherwood as part of the
September 2012 Paintathon fund-raising event. It now hangs in the rebuilt
St Luke's Canning Crescent, Oxford. PHOTO JW

FOREWORD

Quietly, without, on the whole, a great deal of fuss, we are currently seeing the greatest alterations to the interiors of our churches since the late nineteenth century.

Sixty years ago changes were already taking place through the influence of the Parish Communion Movement. The high altar was relegated to only occasional use and was replaced by one in the nave. The pews or chairs were often grouped round it in a horseshoe to stress that the people of God were meeting round the Lord's Table. God's immanence was being stressed as a counter-balance to those of our forebears who had wanted to underline his transcendence.

But in the last few decades something new has been happening. The numerous new heating, sound and lighting systems, serveries and toilets that are being put into churches, coupled with the creation of smaller rooms and chapels within the larger curtilage, come from fresh theological thinking.

First, all of these are designed to assist our congregations in their worship and mission. Our church buildings become places where we meet one another, often after the formal liturgy is completed, into which we feel comfortable about introducing others. To be that they need to be warm and welcoming, while retaining that sense of stillness and the awareness of God that so many long for.

But, secondly, many Church Councils also want them to be the places that are shared with the wider community on every day of the week, and are not the exclusive domain of those who worship in them on a Sunday.

In many ways this can be described as the 're-medievalisation' of our churches. After all, it was our Victorian ancestors who filled what were often empty, flexible spaces with pews and who framed the worship within them in a particular way. In contrast to this, when they were originally built, churches performed a large number of functions in the life of the community, whether as schools or gathering places, and it is no accident that, as a result, many of our village halls, which fulfil many of these functions, date from the late nineteenth and early twentieth centuries. The resultant divide between the secular and the spiritual was very pronounced and, in some cases, very damaging. All too often communities lost the sense that it was their church and felt that it belonged to others. What we are now seeing is a reversal of that trend.

In some cases this has resulted in shops and post offices being moved into the church. In many more it is simply that flexible spaces have been created, to be used in a wide variety of ways by all sorts of community groups.

I am very grateful to Becky Payne for chronicling some of these changes here in Oxfordshire, and for the backing of our Historic Churches Trust in the project. My hope is that this book will help Church Councils and others catch a vision for how their church can best serve its community – and how it can be adapted for doing so where that is needed. I believe that we are now at an exciting tipping point where people are beginning to ask, 'Why haven't we got one?' when referring to anything from a toilet to coffee-making facilities; and once that question has been asked, those focusing on the needs of the wider community soon follow.

The Right Revd Colin Fletcher, OBE
Bishop of Dorchester
November 2013

St Mary the Virgin, Charlbury.
Main entrance showing the glass doors decorated with flowers for a wedding,
May 2013. PHOTO BP

INTRODUCTION

Constraints and obstacles to overcome and the road littered with discarded drawings, seemingly insoluble problems, frustrating beyond measure and how many meetings?
Olive Sutcliffe, churchwarden, taken from *A record and memento celebrating the opening of St Agatha Brightwell-cum-Sotwell's church room in 2012*

The churches of Oxfordshire, many of them – though not all – of great age, are beyond value as centres of worship, as the focus of communities great and small and as historic buildings worth preserving for their beauty as well as what they tell us about our past.

The enormous challenge that most of them face in the twenty-first century is how to make them relevant to an increasingly secularised society, while retaining their numinous quality as sacred spaces. In this book I have examined twenty-five examples of successful adaptation and modernisation, and show how this has been achieved.

The book grew out of an initiative by the Rt Revd Colin Fletcher, Bishop of Dorchester, in partnership with the Oxfordshire Historic Churches Trust, who felt that it was important to record these successes as a way of inspiring others to take up the challenge. The aim was to look in depth at projects that had been identified as examples of best practice and to describe all stages of each from conception to completion. It is hoped that providing practical information and insight from those who have 'gone before' will help other places of worship across the UK that are forming their own ideas to plan and implement what are very complex community building projects.

To those who took the time to tell me about their projects, I am deeply grateful. I spoke to members of the clergy, churchwardens, fund-raisers, architects and many other committed individuals who have developed and created the most wonderful community projects within our historic places of worship. I asked them not only about what they

had achieved, but about their vision, how they made it happen, how they engaged with the wider community, how they raised the funding, how they dealt with the authorities, what challenges they faced and the lessons they learnt. They described their achievements with rightful pride, but also told me about the periods of despair, the frustrations and the 'I will never, ever agree to undertake anything like this ever again' moments.

Whatever their background, most of them found themselves embarking for the first time on a journey dealing with the complexities of working on what was after all both a church and a community project. This not only brought with it the obvious difficulties involved in adapting an historic building, but required special sensitivity, because these are sacred places for many, greatly loved by their local communities – even if some among them hardly cross the threshold.

These twenty-five projects arose out of a genuine wish to meet modern worship needs along with a wish to open up the building for wider community use. Making changes to a worship space is a delicate matter, as it can challenge many people's expectations of what a church should look like. A balance has to be struck between working with the historic fabric of the building and retaining sacred space while at the same time creating an environment that is welcoming to people who may not share the faith of those worshipping there.

There are many more outstanding projects that have been undertaken across Oxfordshire and we were not able to include them all. The decision was reluctantly made to exclude nationally known projects such as those at Dorchester Abbey,* where an outstanding educational, musical and community resource has been created, and at the University Church of St Mary the Virgin, which has recently undertaken a major programme of restoration works and interpretation for visitors. We wanted to focus on smaller, more typical, parish churches and chose cases that represented a range of different solutions – from major reorderings to the installation of a toilet and small servery, from extensions to fitting the new facilities within the base of the west end tower. Even though each project developed out of particular sets of needs and circumstances, a lot of the challenges were common to many.

Agreeing alterations and the location and design of new facilities takes time and involves detailed consultation with the relevant authorities. A Parochial Church Council (PCC) will find that many organisations have an interest in the building and an opinion on its reordering.

Finding out that you cannot do exactly what you had originally envisioned can be a hurdle, and yet I came across much praise for the Diocesan Advisory Committee (DAC) and English Heritage and an appreciation of the advice and guidance they can offer, especially on what may initially appear an insoluble problem.† There is also increased awareness that churches should involve their church authorities and English Heritage as early as possible.

Amenity societies, especially the Victorian

Society, attracted the most flak. This is not surprising, as most of the changes involved altering the nineteenth-century internal arrangements and removing furnishings installed as part of the widespread Victorian restoration of our parish churches. It can seem illogical to a PCC trying to create a more open and sustainable building that it can be prevented from doing so, especially in a church that has undergone radical change almost every century since it was built. In fact, the amenity societies can be a source of advice and knowledge and can help prioritise what is important and what can be changed – in a spirit of intelligent compromise. Consulting early is again the key.

Almost all the churches proposing changes faced a degree of opposition. This sometimes came from within the PCC itself, sometimes from parts of the congregation and sometimes from the wider community. Occasionally it came from all three. As you will read, PCCs tried very hard to communicate and consult by putting questionnaires through every door, asking for suggestions on what uses the community would like to see in the church, putting plans and drawings on public display, holding open meetings and providing regular updates through newsletters and websites. Alongside the many positive responses, PCCs also received expressions of genuine concern and, in some cases, downright hostility. In a small community, any form of opposition can be painful. Some of this comes from a

---

* See *Dorchester Abbey: Church and People 635–2005*, ed. Kate Tiller, pp. 94–109; Stonesfield Press, 2005 (ISBN 0 9527126 4 4).

† PCC and DAC are Anglican terms, but for brevity I also use them to refer to the bodies responsible for churches of other denominations.

fear of change and people's expectations about what they should see in a church. Some is about the fear of losing the special atmosphere when the 'traditional look' has disappeared. There is also difficulty, if you are not used to looking at plans, in visualising what the end result will look like.

PCCs and incumbents said that they listened, talked things through and even amended original proposals, but that in the end they had to take a decision even if it felt like a lonely one. They were the ones faced with the responsibility of looking after an historic building and wondering if it would survive as a place of worship. But there are also many happy endings, where the finished building is greeted with appreciative enthusiasm. As one vicar said, 'If you carry the majority with you, then hopefully more will come on board and others come round when they see the finished result.'

The PCCs involved in these twenty-five cases raised hundreds of thousands of pounds through a combination of congregational giving, local fund-raising and grant applications. For some of the small churches the process can take years, especially if unforeseen problems result in additional works and therefore costs. A big frustration is that all the funders ask for similar information but in slightly different formats; keeping track of the different conditions and monitoring requirements of the various grant-awarding bodies requires the dedication of someone with financial skills, experience and meticulous attention to detail.

Fund-raising through organising events can be exhausting, but all recognised that events are an invaluable way of engaging with the wider community and keeping them informed about the project. Events encourage a feeling of community ownership and even those who don't come to church will still support the building.

Two final challenges come about once the project is completed, but really need to be thought about at all stages of its development.

There may have been a shared vision, but it may take a while to adjust to the new reality of a building that is truly a place of worship and embraces the wider community. As one vicar said, 'All of a sudden people wanted to come into it and use it for non-religious purposes and that is great, but it does lead to some complexity and negotiation.' If a church is able to raise all the money itself, it can regulate the use of the building, but if it has genuinely gone into a partnership with the wider community and asked them for their views and money and they have given freely of both, then, as another vicar said, 'You have to be very sure that your vision for the new building encompasses the new ways in which the building will be used.'

Once the project is finished, PCCs have to evaluate to what extent it is meeting the original objectives. This can include an increase in footfall and income, new people joining the worshipping community, a stronger relationship with the non-churchgoing community, becoming a successful cultural venue, helping to deliver a community service, increased community well-being or even the realisation that more people now value the church and will help to maintain it.

Disappointment was expressed by those whose hopes that the project would increase the congregation size had not necessarily come to pass. Some are also finding that their new building is not being used as much as they hoped and are learning how to market it better and encourage people to use it. Others, although their building is being used a lot, are still uncertain about whether this wider use is going to bring in sufficient income to help sustain the building in the long term. They don't want the church to be seen as a money-making organisation and so don't always charge commercial rates, but running costs have increased. Managing a building with daily activities involves extra administration, not least the effort of setting up and clearing away for different activities. This emphasises the importance of including the costs of managing the 'new' building in the original business plan. Also key is succession planning. Those developing the project and taking it through to completion may well be exhausted. Those managing the established project may well need different skills, so it's important to keep encouraging new volunteers to come on board.

Further research is needed to look at whether and how we can measure what these projects are delivering. Knowing more about the potential benefits of opening up their church while being aware of the practical realities and what outcomes it is reasonable to expect will help the managers of future projects to take the necessary steps to ensure they maximise their success.

After reading the case studies, I hope you will appreciate even more what these projects have achieved and will feel that there is good reason for optimism about the future of our churches. They give us plenty of examples of PCCs and congregations working alongside people from the local community, with tenacity and imagination. They show the huge amounts of time and money these people are prepared to give to ensure that their churches are open as places of worship and that there are more people 'crossing the threshold' to make use of and connect with the building. It is their efforts that will, we hope, build towards providing a sustainable future for the worshipping community and their buildings. Importantly, these are all churches that continue to offer their local communities a place for quiet reflection, an inspiring building and a community space for a whole range of activities.

Becky Payne

St Helen's, Abingdon. Isis Chamber Orchestra rehearsing using the dais. PHOTO STEPHEN THOMAS

St Helen, Abingdon

We looked into the history of our church and found that every generation had its own vision which determined how it laid out the building. We felt we were honouring this historic tradition by making it work for our generation. We have tried to be both backward- and forward-looking. Stephen Thomas, member of the Fabric Committee and former churchwarden

Abingdon is a market town about six miles south of Oxford in the Vale of White Horse district. The third largest market town in Oxfordshire, it has a population of 33,000. St Helen's, the town's civic church, is situated by the River Thames and has a beautiful tapering spire that can be seen for miles.

This Grade 1 listed church is the second widest in England and is almost square in shape, with four aisles either side of the nave as wealthy parishioners added to it over the centuries. Although its origins are in the seventh century the present building dates from the thirteenth. Significant remodelling was carried out from the fifteenth to the eighteenth centuries. It was restored and again reordered between 1873 and 1897 by the architect Henry Woodyer.

THE PROJECT

In 2004 the most recent reordering introduced a nave altar on a raised dais. While three quarters of the pews were retained, they were rearranged so that they now face the altar on three sides. Underfloor heating was installed under a new floor and the pews removed from the south aisle to provide a space for community activities. Access was improved by levelling the paved area outside the main (north) entrance and putting an internal ramp inside the door.

Installing a new sound system was part of the original 2004 plan, but has had to be put on hold because of limited funds. In 2005 the pipe organ was reconditioned, reflecting the importance of the choir and music to the church. In 2010 a kitchen was built in the south porch. In late 2012 new toilets, one fully accessible, were installed just off the north porch between the inner and outer doors.

REALISATION

The main aim of the 2004 reordering was to encourage the renewal of the congregation by creating a more sympathetic worshipping space. Because the church is so wide and was full of pews all facing eastwards, the only people who could see the high altar in the chancel were those sitting in the central nave. The current incumbent, the Revd Charles Miller, who arrived after the reordering, said, 'It would have been a pretty immobile sacred space with impediments to any other kind of alternative movements beyond just coming into your pew and going to communion.' Stephen Thomas describes how, during services, there were 'what I call "simultaneous acts of private devotion" rather than people collectively around the Lord's Table. The congregation was separated physically, visually and audibly and felt unconnected.'

The PCC and the previous incumbent, the Revd Michael Goode, worked with the architect Robert Maguire of Maguire and Co. to develop a scheme that was more communitarian in nature. A nave altar, made of simple white oak, was placed on a raised dais that projects into the centre of the church. The dais, which is about 15cm high, reuses some of the tiles from the Victorian floor, now replaced.

Before the installation of the underfloor heating and new floor, the Victorian pews were taken out and stored. Three quarters were put back, some of them shortened, and rearranged in what is still a very formal way, but rotated to form a

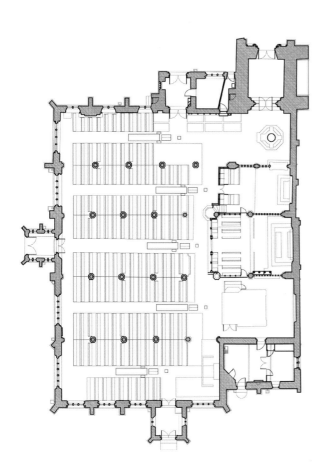

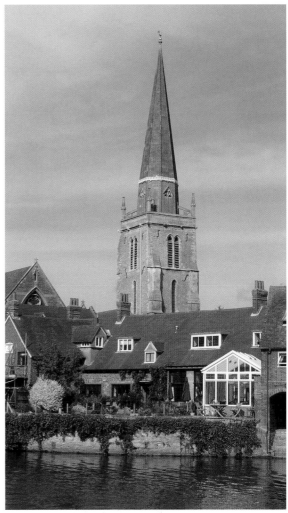

Top right The spectacular spire rising above the rooftops, August 2005. PHOTO JW

Above Plan showing the layout of the pews before the 2004 reordering. PHOTO JBKS ARCHITECTS

Right From west end towards east end, the nave altar raised on a dais and the double corona, July 2013. PHOTO BP

Above Concert rehearsal in the south aisle, February 2006.
PHOTO STEPHEN THOMAS

Left Looking across to the north entrance with pews in the north aisle facing south to offer a clear view of the nave altar. PHOTO BP

u shape. As the visitors' guide says, 'like a theatrical thrust stage, the nave altar area is now fully visible to the congregation which surrounds the altar on three sides'.

The Revd Charles Miller says, 'We had the opportunity to become a community as we would essentially be worshipping, looking at one another across the various trajectories with the altar more or less in the centre. And I think that a sense of community, fellowship and solidarity has in fact been engendered by the reorientation of the space.' A delicate corona, designed by Robert Maguire, hangs over and lights the new altar, establishing it as a place of significance. By focusing on the new altar it draws the eye away from the original high altar.

The chancel was unchanged and is used for small services. In the early 1980s the PCC had sought to remove the rood screen, but there had been strong opposition from the DAC. In 1986, the matter went to a Consistory Court, at which a faculty was refused. The screen is now seen as a benefit separating the new altar from the chancel, which functions as a small chapel. Turning the lights down in the chancel during the main services means it does not distract from the new altar. At the same Consistory Court, a faculty was granted to permit the removal of some pews and to permit the removal of others for a trial period of five years.

The second priority for the PCC was to create an area that could be used by the community. Abingdon does have some performance spaces, but only one, the Guild Hall, belongs to the town. The south aisle, the last to be constructed, just before the Reformation, was opened up and left empty of pews. Instead 300 stackable chairs were purchased which are put out for large services, but otherwise it is kept clear for exhibitions, social gatherings and concerts.

The retained pews have been refurbished. Remounted on rubber feet and just resting on the new tile floor, they are much more mobile. While originally the screwed-down pews could be moved, it was a lengthy business. 'It took hours to get them back after a concert and they never fitted back perfectly,' says Stephen Thomas. 'We did have a consultation and the strongest feedback came from families with young children who prefer pews to

chairs as they provide a good contained play area.' They have created a children's area by arranging seven pews in a square around a column at the west end of the north aisle.

In 2010 a kitchen was installed in the south porch, and is convenient for activities in the south aisle. In 2012 toilets were put in just off the north porch main entrance, alongside a small office space. This was part of a project to refurbish the Exchequer Room above the north porch, which had been built by the medieval fraternity of the Holy Cross. A £40,000 grant from the Oxfordshire Historic Churches Trust paid for the initial refurbishment, offering the chance to install the toilets below. The Exchequer Room is still being developed and will be used as a workroom.

Providing disabled access was a challenge because of different levels but it was resolved by building an internal ramp just inside the main north door. An added benefit for visitors entering the church is that they find themselves on a small platform, allowing them to see the whole space and orientate themselves.

Planning for these changes goes back twenty years. In 1995 a temporary nave altar was set up to see how it might work. Between 1995 and 2000, the PCC undertook a wide-reaching consultation, meeting representatives of the local council and local orchestras and community groups to ask for their thoughts on how the church could be used. They also talked to the DAC, the Victorian Society and several architects. They collated the feedback into a single document, which was given to Maguire and Co., a firm chosen because of the strong Christian mission that informs their work. They took part in worship and attended concerts so that they could experience the space.

Stephen Thomas remembers that about half the congregation had strong reservations, and going ahead with the project was controversial. People were worried that changing the orientation of the pews was abandoning 700 or 800 years of history. The PCC encouraged research into the church's history to show that the pews had in fact only been around for the last 130 years and that there had been at least four major reorderings. Others felt that it didn't work as a modern worship space and wanted to do things differently.

Access ramp inside the north entrance, and pews in the north aisle turned to face south, July 2013. PHOTO BP

Toilets and office space leading off from the north porch between the inner and outer doors, July 2013. PHOTO BP

Children's area in the north-west corner, July 2013. PHOTO BP

The PCC and congregation are very pleased with the changes. Because so many pews were retained and the new arrangement is still formal, Stephen Thomas says that visitors are often surprised that the layout is only eight or nine years old.

The project cost about £1 million. About two thirds of that came from the congregation, the rest from the sale of a curate's house and some grants. Stephen Thomas says, 'There was some amazing generosity including from some people who said "I can't agree with the reordering, but I will actually support this because I can see it is going to help the church long-term."' The work was phased over ten years, with fund-raising throughout, and the different elements were treated as separate projects with different contractors. The PCC is currently investigating whether it can put in a new lighting system, which would provide additional help for theatrical productions and exhibitions.

Since the reordering there have been numerous concerts, using both the south aisle and the dais. The raised dais and the lighting are beneficial for performances. The dais can be emptied and the movable altar-rails stowed away to provide a large performing space. The corona supplies lighting focused on to the performers.

'Previously,' says Stephen Thomas, 'we were having a concert only every five years, but it is now bringing in new audiences and new performers.' Especially memorable was a concert by the local brass band, which attracted people who said they had lived in Abingdon for fifty years, but had never set foot in St Helen's before as they felt that if they weren't worshipping they shouldn't go in. The church now offers one of the largest venues in the area and hosts concerts of 600, 200 in an orchestra or a choir and 400 in the audience. Mr Thomas says their record is over 700 'and that is Abingdon School, as we are the only local venue that can accommodate the whole school'. It is also used for community dances, large dinner parties, children's parties and exhibitions.

There have been other unexpected benefits. For funerals, a gathering of family and friends can take place in the south aisle after a service while the coffin is taken to the baptistery in the north side of the church. Later the undertakers return and the family can go with the coffin to the crematorium.

The PCC and incumbent are now looking at how they can ensure that the changes deliver the envisaged outcomes. They have had to adjust to the building's being used for both sacred and secular purposes. Mr Miller says, 'Some people using the space have no sense of its sacredness and it's a real shock the first time you see a can of Coca Cola put down on the altar table. It's an issue that requires vigilance and one we have to negotiate for the greater good.'

They are currently unsure of how much the additional uses are contributing to the mission of the church and the sustainability of the building. Currently these do bring in an income, but Mr Miller feels that the PCC is not currently able to make the most of the potential created by the reordered space and the opportunities for building new relationships with the community. It does not have the capacity to administer, manage and generate much more usage and appointing a paid programme developer is not something it can currently afford.

Mr Miller feels that opening up a church for community use should not be seen as a guarantee of increasing a congregation. 'More people are coming into the church, but they are coming in for events and the notion that maybe they will be struck with the truth of the Gospel doesn't usually happen.'

CHALLENGES
Change is difficult to manage, but don't be put off by initial reservations. If you consult widely and listen to people, you can move forward.

LESSON LEARNED
Start with your vision rather than with the building. You are then more likely to achieve your objectives.

BEST PIECE OF ADVICE
Ensure you understand the fundamental theological sense of why your church exists and then there will be all sorts of scope.

WEBSITE
http://sthelenabingdon.cloudaccess.net

TRINITY CHURCH, ABINGDON

As part of our service to the community, Trinity Church and the Conduit Centre premises are used by a great number of people during each week. Church website

Abingdon is a market town near Oxford (see St Helen, Abingdon). Trinity Church in Conduit Road, close to the centre of the town, was built as a new Methodist church in 1875 when the existing chapel had become overcrowded. Unlisted, it has a 128ft-high spire and its interior consists of a sanctuary with a Pre-Raphaelite stained-glass window at the east end. In 1968 the Congregationalists (now United Reformed Church) began sharing the building with the Methodists.

There had been a Congregationalist Meeting House in Abingdon since 1700. In 1862 the Congregationalists built a church in the nearby square. As Abingdon grew northwards a new church, All Saints, was built in Appleford Drive in 1959. In time, half the congregation moved to share the nearby Trinity Church and half moved to All Saints. The vacated Congregational Church in the square was put up for sale with the intention that the funds raised would go towards a new church in South Abingdon. However, after planning difficulties the sum realised from the sale did not reach expectations and the plan did not proceed. In 1984 the joint congregation at Trinity decided to use the money to pay for the complete refurbishment of the old Sunday School rooms, creating additional rooms and installing a mezzanine floor. The building was renamed the Conduit Centre.

The church is now a local ecumenical project and members of Trinity come from many different backgrounds.

THE PROJECT

Trinity Church is very community-focused and reaches out to the wider population in many ways. It has two large buildings, which are used for the church's own programme and as part of its service to the community, for a large number of activities.

REALISATION

The main church building, with its flexible seating arrangement for up to 300 people, is often used for public concerts and school events along with many christenings, weddings and funerals. In the 1990s a fully accessible set of toilets was put in near the entrance, as well as a small kitchen. The entrance area was developed to become a Welcome Area, and a mezzanine floor, which can be used as a separate room, was built above it.

About five or six schools use the church for Christmas concerts and the Abingdon Operatic Society uses it for performances. It is a large, airy space, made cheery by its blue walls, yellow carpet tiles and recently installed LED lighting.

The sanctuary area, which was brought forward on a platform, provides a good-sized stage. The seating area is slightly raked, which helps audience visibility.

The church is separated by a lawn and gardens from the Conduit Centre, an extensive hall block with a small adjoining car park. The centre contains a large hall with seating for 150 people. It also has four smaller rooms suitable for meetings of fifteen to thirty people, two offices, and a well equipped kitchen.

Used for meetings by numerous church-linked and church-run groups, the centre attracts a mix

Exterior from the south, August 2005. PHOTO JW

of Trinity churchgoers and non-attenders. The Evergreen Club, which meets monthly for a varied programme of speakers and entertainment, is for older people and offers refreshments and transport to and from their homes. About one third of the club members attend Trinity for Sunday worship.

Other church-related groups include the twice-weekly Toddlers' Group, for which there is a waiting list, a Youth Group, and the Cub Scouts, Scouts, Brownies and Guides, which have weekly meetings and for which there are also waiting lists.

With the proviso that it will not let to a group whose ethos they could not support, the centre hires out space to a wide range of community groups such as the Abingdon Operatic Society, Young Farmers' Club, Stroke Club, tai chi classes, children's music groups, ballet and dance groups, as well as for private parties.

For six years between 2001 and 2007, Trinity Church ran a Trinity Youth Project that employed three people, a Student Youth Worker, an Outreach Worker and an Outreach Coordinator, who worked with young people in the community and local schools. The Outreach Worker worked with the Abingdon Bridge Drop-In Centre, which offered support to young people with personal and social problems. The Youth Project was funded by local and national grants and contributions from the congregation.

Out of this came TrinityLearning, an initiative specific to Trinity Church, which began in October 2009 when an Education & Development Officer, Rosemary Perrow, was appointed. Her remit was to explore ways in which the church could use its time, talents and space to enhance the quality of life for all staff and students in local schools.

Rosemary Perrow says, 'It is not evangelism or chaplaincy, but rather introducing children to the concept of spirituality.' The church has developed a positive partnership with the local primary school, helping it plan a reflective garden and working with children prior to important services. Two of the original projects, Experience Easter and Hello Abingdon, along with supported work experience for secondary school students, are still ongoing and have become increasingly popular. Over the last four years,

children from seventeen schools in the Abingdon area have been involved in these or other projects.

Ms Perrow adds, 'Our work has brought around 2,000 new users to the premises and TrinityLearning has gained recognition as a valid and valuable contributor in the local educational community.'

They are able to support schools in teaching Citizenship and Religious Education as part of Key Stages 1 and 2 for primary schools. Classes come into the church and find out about church signs and symbols and the Christian faith through a range of activities. The most successful activity has been the annual Experience Easter workshops. All the chairs are moved out of the church and over two days about 400 primary schoolchildren experience the events of Easter Week through reflective storytelling and activities around the church.

There has been focus on supporting forces children from Dalton Barracks, two or three miles away. Having to move house frequently, some suffer from a lack of confidence, literacy problems and difficulties in mixing with their peers. Schools in Abingdon reported this as a particular area of concern because the children are divided among many schools, making it difficult for individual schools to help them.

To address this, in November 2010 the TrinityLearning News project was set up. Funded initially by a Big Lottery Fund grant, it has continued with a grant from the Community Covenant grant scheme, which supports local projects working to strengthen the ties and mutual understanding between armed forces families and the wider community in which they live.

The project, using church reprographic equipment, produces a community newspaper. Based at the church and Conduit Centre, it is created by groups of children from local primary schools, half from forces families and half from the local community. It goes out to the barracks and to the schools involved and the aim is to strengthen bonds between the two, while at the same time giving the children a confidence-boosting educational experience. As the introduction to an edition produced in October 2012 by six children from Carswell Primary School says: 'We are writing this newspaper to learn different things that involve the army. We wanted to do this

because the army is very important to Abingdon. Nearly half the people that go to our school have a family member in the army. We were able to visit Dalton Barracks and we spoke to some soldiers, saw some equipment and we interviewed Regimental Sergeant Major David Wakefield.'

Trinity is particularly keen to share the idea of offering work experience placements for secondary school students. 'There are always loads of jobs to be done, from serving teas to pensioners to IT tasks beyond the congregation's skills. Bringing in a student gives them a chance to feel valued and to meet people of faith and brings a breath of fresh air into the church.' In the case of TrinityLearning, experience in mentoring allows them to offer places for students needing that little bit of extra support, who might otherwise find it difficult to obtain a placement.

CHALLENGE
Finding new sources of funding to enable projects to continue is a constant challenge.

WEBSITE
http://www.trinityabingdon.org.uk

Top Interior, August 2005. PHOTO JW

Above The church set up for the Easter Experience, March 2012. PHOTO ROSEMARY PERROW

St Peter and St Paul, Aston Rowant

Our vision is that the Aston Rowant Church Annexe Project (ARCAP) will create a place within this beautiful 900-year-old building which everyone can make use of and enjoy, thus continuing the centuries-old tradition of adapting historic churches to ever-changing needs. Project brochure

A small village in a rural part of south-east Oxfordshire, Aston Rowant lies at the foot of the Chiltern Hills. With a population of about 850, it consists mainly of attractive houses and farms centred around the church and a large village green.

The church of St Peter and St Paul is Grade II* listed, of flint with stone dressings. The original church, probably built in the eleventh century, consisted of a nave and possibly a small chancel, while two small Romanesque windows indicate that an earlier place of worship probably existed on the site. Following several periods of reconstruction and improvement, it now comprises a nave with chapels on the north and south sides, a chancel, a south porch, and a west tower. The architect E. G. Bruton undertook a thorough restoration in 1884.

THE PROJECT

Between September 2011 and February 2012, the PCC added a new annexe to the north side of the church containing a fully accessible modern kitchen and toilet, and refurbished the fourteenth-century Lady Chapel to provide a spacious and comfortable function area. With fitted carpets, a table and upholstered seating and a floor space of 35sqm, it offers a flexible space and village centre for the congregation and residents alike.

REALISATION

The village shop and pub closed some years ago, leaving no community facility. St Peter and St Paul was in a good state of repair and had been completely redecorated internally in 2003.

The church is open during daylight hours all year round and is much visited by tourists, historians and people searching for ancestors' graves. And the work made sense for the church, too. It was already very popular for weddings; one of the first questions guests who had travelled long distances would ask was 'where is the toilet?' It was felt it was no longer sufficient to rely on helpful neighbours to provide those facilities.

Much discussion at parish meetings brought such comments as 'the church has stood here for 900 years without a toilet – why does it need one now?' Finally, agreed by the full PCC that it was needed, the ARCAP subcommittee was formed, which still operates, continuing to look after maintenance and promote the new facilities for wider use. A bank account was opened and Robert Montgomery Architects were commissioned. The subcommittee started fundraising immediately and, importantly, involved the Archdeacon, the DAC and English Heritage at the earliest opportunity.

Several options were looked at. One was to install the toilet at the base of the tower at the west end, when its roof would provide a new platform for the bell-ringers. However, English Heritage was concerned that in order to ring the full set of bells, the platform would have had to extend beyond the tower footprint. Both English Heritage and the DAC were also concerned that it would cut off light from the west end window. The second option, to install the facility in the south aisle, would have cut off light from the aisle window and there was worry that flushing would be audible during services.

It became clear that the south aisle would be

Exterior from the south-east, September 2005. PHOTO JW

better used as the vestry and the point from where the choir processes. Up until then, there was no vestry and the choir and vicar were both using the very small room off the chancel that contained the boiler.

This left the north aisle, the Lady Chapel. It was first thought that a toilet could go behind the organ, but this would have cut off light from the west window and it would have again required soundproofing. However, by this time, it had been agreed that a kitchen was needed, with a space to make full use of the planned facilities.

It became clear that the kitchen and toilet should be installed in an annexe leading from the north door and that the community space could be provided in the Lady Chapel in front of the organ. The chapel was filled with pews fashioned out of recycled sixteenth- or seventeenth-century panelling, the floor was in a terrible state, and the area had become a dumping-ground. Anyone seated there had to rely on the squint in order to see the chancel and high altar.

It was decided to remove the existing pews and pew platform in the Lady Chapel to provide a level, clear floor area in line with the existing timber floor. The church authorities were definite that they did not want to close off this space using screens, not only because it would have meant enclosing the organ, but because they saw no need to separate the community space from worship space.

Consideration was given to taking out all the pews from the nave at the same time, but it was decided that this was a step too far.

The architect was asked to produce two designs, one traditional and one contemporary. The DAC and English Heritage were consulted on both and a big display with plans and drawings was put up in the church. Members of the congregation were invited at the end of every service to have a look and make comments and local residents were specifically invited to give feedback.

Reactions were divided between those who wanted the church to look traditional and those who felt that, as there had been many previous changes throughout its history, it made sense to continue that process and bring it into the twenty-first century. Cost also came into it, as the price of the

contemporary design was half that of the traditional one. English Heritage stressed that 'the success of the proposal will to a great extent be dependent on the quality of materials selected and the workmanship of the proposed flint of the building'. The DAC was supportive of both options and left it to the PCC, who decided to go with the contemporary version.

In fact, the resulting annexe is of very good quality, in both design and workmanship, and fits in very well with the original building. The only intervention required in the fabric of the church was to sort out adequate drainage. A small penetration into the north wall provided power and water supplies to the proposed annexe, which is now mostly screened by mature yew trees and other bushes and shrubs.

The annexe is constructed of flint walls with stone dressings to match the existing church walls. The only modern external feature is the two long hardwood-framed rectangular windows at the junction of the new and existing walls. The windows are set back into the structure in order to provide natural light into the kitchenette and the toilet, the latter, with disabled access, fitted with obscured glass. The roof is a shallow-pitched timber structure covered with natural slate to match the existing church roofing, with conservation roof windows to provide additional daylight.

The opportunity was taken to improve access to the whole building, an important consideration. Previously entry was gained via the south porch, but the two sets of steps made it impossible for wheelchair users. They can now enter via the west door at the base of the tower. There was a small step at this location but a temporary ramp will give level access through the tower into the nave and in the long term the step will be removed. A ramp has been created at a gradient of 1:12 to enable access from the nave to the community space and annexe, which are 110mm higher. The higher ground level outside on the north side meant there was a step up to the north door, and the organ was on a plinth, so the decision was made to raise the whole north aisle floor to match the existing level of the north door.

Before deciding upon furniture, the PCC went to look at other churches where new chairs had been

Right The new annexe on the north side of the church, July 2013. PHOTO JW

Below The new facilities in the annexe seen through the door leading from the north aisle, July 2013. The entrance to the toilet is on the left. PHOTO JW

Bottom right A parish supper taking place in the new community space using the new chairs, July 2013. PHOTO JOHN WYATT

installed and especially liked stacking chairs from America. The tables too were chosen on the basis that they are stackable and light to move around. Cupboards were installed along the north wall of the north aisle alongside the organ to store flower-arranging materials and equipment for the new sound system.

All the pews removed from the Lady Chapel were relocated at the back of the nave pews at the west end, where they are required for big weddings and special services.

The committee produced a presentation brochure which made the case for the project and included photographs and drawings of the proposed annexe.

The total cost of the project came to £110,000. Fund-raising took about three months and consisted of four strands. The committee wrote personal letters to individuals in the village: this raised 28% of the total in two weeks. A villager in contact with the Garfield Weston Foundation helped raise a grant that made up 30% and an Oxfordshire Historic Churches Trust grant provided 9% of the total. A meeting was also held with the South Oxfordshire District Council (SODC) and its members were all given a hard copy of the presentation brochure to read at leisure rather than as a powerpoint presentation. They agreed to provide a grant from their Community Trust to make up the shortfall.

All funding bids concentrated on the fact that there is no village hall or other facilities in Aston Rowant and that this was going to be a community space for the whole village.

The new annexe was launched with an Open Day in April 2012. ARCAP produced a brochure called Your Space which was put through every door in the village, inviting everyone to visit the centre and to share their thoughts on 'what you would like to do, and see to be done, in your Community Centre'.

Since then, the space has been used for meetings of the Parish Council and the Women's Institute, among others. The church can now provide refreshments for concerts, and parties for community baptisms can now be held there.

The congregation has benefited: previously they had after-service coffee at the west end in front of the font, where the only seating was in the pews.

Now they have comfortable and movable chairs, much appreciated by the elderly members of the congregation.

By locating the facilities in an annexe, the church has retained much of its original feel. The high altar is still used and, looking towards the chancel from the west end, nothing much has changed.

The PCC may consider other changes in the future, but at the moment its members are enjoying the new space and concentrating on encouraging new users. The most immediate issue is deciding upon a long-term name for the community space that reflects its purpose and its new users.

CHALLENGES
Concern about the changes was addressed by making time for discussion and explaining the need for facilities. A key issue was the need to provide for the future financial sustainability of the church.

LESSONS LEARNED
Before they started, the members of ARCAP visited another church that had recently completed an annexe and asked them to share their experiences. Their overall response was that the difficulty was not so much the finance, but the bureaucracy. Their advice: involve the Archdeacon and DAC at an early stage and seek advice at every stage thereafter.

BEST PIECE OF ADVICE
If you are thinking of developing any major project spend time and money on a brochure that sets out your vision and use photos and plans to describe your proposal. This enables all interested parties including local people, secular and church authorities and grant-givers to understand the project and it demonstrates your commitment.

WEBSITE
https://sites.google.com/site/stpeterandstpaulastonrowant/home

St Edburg, Bicester

Dear God, we remember with gratitude those who built, repaired and adapted St Edburg's Church for over 900 years. As we work to tackle the building challenges of our generation, we ask for your grace and hope; we ask for courage and determination. We trust in you to enable us to deliver work worthy of the place where we worship and serve you, almighty God; through Jesus Christ our Lord. Amen. A prayer written by the Revd Maggie Durran and used regularly by the congregation of St Edburg's during the building project (a number of prayers relating to the building works are available on the church's website)

Bicester is an historic market town in north-east Oxfordshire. Recorded in the Domesday Book, today it is probably best known for Bicester Village, the designer outlet shopping centre situated a mere five-minute walk from the town. With a current population of about 32,000, it is one of the fastest-growing towns in the UK, benefiting from its proximity to the M40 linking London with Birmingham via Oxford. St Edburg's parish church is in the centre at the end of Church Street, just off the Market Place.

It is generally believed that the Grade I listed church of St Edburg was built in 1104, replacing an earlier Saxon church. By the thirteenth century the Norman cross-shaped church had been given to Bicester Priory and was enlarged several times by the addition of the thirteenth-century south aisle, fourteenth-century north aisle and choir vestry, and the fifteenth-century tower. The church was restored in 1862–63 by the architect C. N. Beazley in consultation with G. E. Street. The roofs and walls were repaired, the floor of the nave was lowered, the whole church was completely retiled and the eighteenth-century box pews and galleries were replaced with the current bench pews.

THE PROJECT

In June 2008 St Edburg's embarked on a multi-stage reordering project. The work has been carefully phased: initially the church was redecorated and rewired throughout and new lighting installed. The next phase, to install toilets and servery facilities at the west end, is due to start early in 2014. The final phase will involve removing the pews and their platforms, putting down a new limestone floor and bringing in chairs and tables. The entire project will cost over £1 million.

REALISATION

Visitors are always impressed by this large, airy church and its high oak roof. As the largest non-commercial covered area in Bicester, it has always been used for community events. However, it had been run down for some years and was threatened with closure, if temporary, because of dangerous electrical fittings.

The PCC had been slowly making plans. There was enthusiasm for reordering as early as 2000, but then things drifted. Churchwarden Diana Pettifer says, 'There was a long lead-in time and we probably did not move quickly enough from theoretical to getting things done. Some of the impetus was lost.'

The arrival of the new vicar, the Revd Canon Theresa Scott, was instrumental in developing a practical reordering strategy. Importantly, she helped make the link between refurbishing the building and the church's mission to better serve the community. She also instilled confidence that it could be achieved and that the money could be raised.

The vision, says Diana Pettifer, was to make the building more versatile to reflect the 'way we worship and also to make it less alien to newcomers and not just church attenders. We want the building to increase the ways we can serve the community, and more people and groups to use it. It was important that any changes made also kept the essential architectural and historical features of the building. We want people to see that it is not just an historical building, but of real relevance to Bicester residents' lives.'

Phase I, completed in 2009, involved the redecoration and rewiring of the interior, enabling the installation of an audio-visual system. A new lighting system was specially designed and displays the architecture of the church at its best. It incorporates digital scene-set control, which can specify lighting for a range of activities from church services to tourism and concerts. This phase cost £200,000, which was raised largely through local events such as a Charity Ball, and a few small grants.

Seeing the cleaned and repainted interior has given renewed energy to the team. 'We've all noticed new things about the building, including the twelve fine stone corbels, carved heads of beasts and grotesques that support the roof structure,' says Janette Hathaway, deputy churchwarden.

Unfortunately, the redecorating works revealed a serious problem of wet and dry rot in the vestry at the east end of the north aisle. 'For months', says Janette Hathaway, 'we had the "swimming pool" as a feature of this area until the necessary additional £85,000 could be accumulated to repair the damage and construct a new drain outside.' They took the opportunity to relay the floor with new stone and install underfloor heating, which will be laid throughout the rest of the church as part of Phase 3.

For Phase 2, the plan is to install at the west end two toilets in the north aisle and a servery in the south aisle. The font currently in the north aisle will be moved to the west end, which will enable more people to participate in baptisms. Led by architects Acanthus Clews, this phase will cost around £220,000.

The final phase, estimated to cost £500,000, will be the most expensive and will make the most visible difference. The pews and their platforms will be removed and replaced by chairs and tables. The Victorian tiled floor will be taken up, and underfloor heating will be extended throughout the church under a new floor, level throughout, of Creeton limestone.

The Victorian Society were initially concerned about the plans, but changed their minds after the PCC insisted they came to visit. Once they had

seen the poor-quality 1860s pine bench pews and their platforms and the all-pervasive presence of woodworm, they agreed to the changes on condition that the stone pulpit from 1863 was retained. The chancel has been redecorated and will be left as it is, complete with Victorian seating and tiled floor.

Prior to applying for a faculty, an archaeological investigation took place, during which four holes were dug in the nave and aisles to ascertain the pre-Victorian floor levels.

The PCC undertook a thorough consultation on all the proposed changes before repairing the vestry. It individually contacted existing users, residents and local businesses, explained the proposals and asked for suggestions of wider uses for the church. There was some initial concern about the pews from non-attenders, otherwise 100% of those who responded wanted to see the church more used and better able to serve the town.

Raising £1 million has been the biggest challenge. Phasing the work has enabled the fund-raising to be divided up into achievable milestones. The PCC started with the congregation, which was important as a way of showing the wider community and grant bodies the commitment of the church itself to the project.

A group of church members and Bicester residents set up the St Edburg's Foundation to encourage support from those in the town 'who may not be members of the church, but who value this ancient building and appreciate its contribution to Bicester, and who believe it is important to sustain and enhance its heritage among the wider community as well as enabling it to meet the needs of today's community in ways old and new'.

The church and the Foundation together and separately have organised plenty of fund-raising events such as concerts, craft fairs, art festivals in the church, golf days and gala dinners. Two items particularly captured the imagination of local residents.

The Heritage Box is a plan to bury a stainless steel box under the font when it is moved to its new position. Over the winter of 2012–13, local residents, in return for a donation, were invited to write personal messages on archival paper for future

Right Exterior from the south-east, June 2006. PHOTO JW

Below Existing kitchen facilities at the base of the tower, July 2013. PHOTO BP

Below right Interior looking towards the east end, showing pews, new lighting and audio-visual system, and Victorian tiled floor, January 2012. PHOTO JW

generations. There were several open days which generated a very good response, especially from children.

In July 2012, the St Edburg's Foundation organised a Living History Day. A series of tableaux added colour to the history of Bicester Priory and the church. Most popular were a very grumpy Henry VIII, played by the new Deacon, and the Victorian lady in the churchyard telling visitors about the victims of the 1832 cholera epidemic.

A recent appeal to the congregation for short-term loans (three years) has been very successful and will enable Phase 2, the installation of toilets and servery, to start early in 2014 and be completed by the middle of the year.

Sadly, the last quinquennial inspection revealed the need for urgent stonework repairs and a new drainage system, which is likely to cost an additional £280,000. The church has therefore recently been added to the English Heritage At Risk Register. Diana Pettifer says, 'We have now got to the point where we have exhausted local resources and will have to apply to the larger grant-giving bodies.'

Worship is set to continue using the nave altar and it is expected that having chairs will allow much more flexibility for services, especially for the 9.30am Sunday Family Service, numbers for which are growing.

The new facilities will increase the potential for church use. Currently there is only a small sink at

The chancel fully scaffolded during Phase 1 works,
September 2009. PHOTO MATTHEW HATHAWAY

Living History Day and the Victorian lady with the memorial
to the victims of the 1832 cholera epidemic, July 2012.
PHOTO MATTHEW HATHAWAY

the base of the tower, and the toilets and cooker are
about a hundred yards away in the 1970s church hall.
The hall houses the parish office and is already hired
out to full capacity for church and other groups.

Many groups have expressed an interest in using
the church and PCC members have plenty of ideas:
one is to provide lunches and a networking forum
for local businesses. They also want to improve the
weekly lunches already provided for the homeless.
They hope it will mean that the church can be kept
open for longer than just mornings.

CHALLENGES
Fund-raising. A fund-raiser for a large project
can be essential, but at the very least do get
some advice or training and ensure it covers the
particular needs of places of worship.

Everything takes longer than you think,
especially processes such as obtaining a faculty.
So always give important stages more than
enough time.

LESSONS LEARNED
Raise your profile in whatever positive ways you
can. The Heritage Box was picked up by the local
media and generated a lot of publicity for the
restoration project.

The relationship you have with your architect
is very important. It is an advantage to have a

local person who can more easily attend meetings
or urgent site meetings.

Expect the unexpected, such as archaeological
investigations or additional problems revealed by
the works, which will undoubtedly require more
time and money.

BEST PIECES OF ADVICE
Visit other churches to get ideas, but it is
important that you develop your own proposals
which are specific to your situation and are
appropriate for your own building.

The vicar does not need to run the project,
but can play a vital role in articulating the vision
and in helping the project team and congregation
to keep hold of that vision during a sometimes
lengthy project.

Ensure that users of the church are alerted in
good time to the potential disruption that building
work may cause. There is a fine line between
doing this well ahead of the scheduled work, and
possibly losing bookings needlessly if the work is
delayed.

WEBSITE
http://www.stedburgschurch.org/

St Agatha, Brightwell-cum-Sotwell

Community projects are not just about buildings – even builders agree! The project team integrates with the community during the span of each project and these relationships remain long after the work terminates. The sentiment for and the great memories from our community builds fortify the feeling of satisfaction at a 'job well done'.

Anna Dulnikowska-Przystalska, director at WALLtd

Brightwell-cum-Sotwell is a twin village in the Upper Thames Valley in South Oxfordshire. Formerly separate villages, Brightwell and Sotwell meet in the very long and winding main street. St Agatha's and the village hall face each other at the Brightwell end in the heart of the village, near the war memorial and some of the oldest houses. The population is about 1,550 and the lively village website presents a picture of an active, thrivingcommunity, which has a volunteer-run village shop with a satellite post office.

Listed Grade II*, the original church was built in 1153 with a dedication, rare in England, to St Agatha. The chancel was rebuilt and aisles added in the fourteenth century. The tower fell down in 1796 and was rebuilt in brick the following year. The nave ceiling was replaced in 1815 and the church further restored in 1858 by Benjamin Ferrey, who organized the removal of the pews and west gallery and had the altar raised on steps. In 1888 the chancel ceiling was removed, exposing the medieval timbers.

THE PROJECT

Between April and September 2012, an extension was built to serve as a 4 x 7m multi-function room with a servery. Access is through the church's south door into a porch-style link. This houses two toilets, one for disabled use, operated using an environmentally friendly and sustainable trench archway system. Both the link and the extension have separate external access to allow them to be used independently of the main church.

The original design was initiated by David Birkett Architect with the assistance, in the later design stage, of Anna Dulnikowska-Przystalska. Anna then managed the project to completion as a director of WALLtd.

REALISATION

In 2004, Brightwell-cum-Sotwell was one of the first parishes in England to publish a Community Led Parish Plan setting out a vision of how the parish should evolve over the next decade. This recognised that the Grade II* listed church was an important part of the local heritage that needed to be sustained, and one of the main priorities was 'developing a new community focus at the church'. An update to the plan in 2006 reported: 'Thursday coffee mornings in St Agatha's have helped to develop the church's role in the community. There is also a proposal to install toilets in St Agatha's to enable the building to be used for community activities.'

Prior to the start of the 2014 Community Plan, an analysis of the 2004 action points reported: 'The community had been looking at ways to foster greater integration of church and community, leading to improved facilities and utilisation of the church, and had been supporting the church in its successful attempts to raise money to build the new Church Room which had opened in September 2012.'

In 2009 the PCC did its own survey, which the Chair of the Building Project Team, David Greasby, says was just to be 'sure we did have the backing of the community'. It went to everybody in the village and there was a good response, 'mainly because we handed the survey to people and then returned to collect it'.

The members of the PCC were clear they wanted

to do something for both the church and the community. The initial fund-raising leaflet said, 'We want to look outwards as well as inwards and with this [proposed] building we hope we can offer something to everyone in our community.'

Various options were studied, among them putting facilities inside the church. This would have meant taking out the choir vestry and possibly some pews at the west end. However, the local school uses the church six times a year for full assemblies, as the only place big enough. For the Revd Jeremy Goulston, who became Team Vicar in 2007, 'in a smallish church, the pews are still the best way of seating a whole primary school or indeed a large congregation', which is the case at some weddings, funerals, baptisms and Christmas and Remembrance services.

There is no space at the base of the tower, which houses the bell chamber, as the eighteenth-century rebuilt tower is considerably shorter than the original. The congregation was already using the empty north aisle to have coffee and socialise after the services, but it was felt that putting in structures housing a toilet and servery would clutter up the building and lose a sense of the internal architectural space.

Mr Goulston felt that a reordering of the church building itself 'was never going to be achievable considering the size of our community and would also perhaps cause such division within the community that we would never achieve resolution. It is a fine judgement and I think what we have now is something we can build on. If in future we are asked whether we want to make the space more flexible inside or do things inside, well, we have a good basis from which to do that.'

Originally, the PCC was thinking of just a porch with toilets, but even a small scheme was going to cost about £50,000–£60,000, so to be cost-effective it made sense to go for a larger building and include a kitchenette and a meeting room. Early on, the DAC and Archdeacon visited and suggested a free-standing building in the churchyard, but the PCC members had decided they wanted the Church Room to be part of the building. The breakthrough came when it was decided that they should focus on the twelfth-century south door. English Heritage, reluctant to allow any other door to be 'knocked through', agreed

that the south door could be used as long as it was not altered in any way. The external doors to the porch-like link into the extension and the south door out of it are all glass, so there is always a view of the twelfth-century door and a visual reminder of the church beyond.

The traditional design chosen, clad in Bath rubblestone, is sensitive to the fabric of the church. Situated on the south side opposite the north main entrance, it still allows the old structure to dominate.

A tarmac path takes wheelchairs right to the extension entrance. A local nursing home brings residents for Wednesday morning coffee, easier now that they can drive closer to the entrance.

Inside, the extension is light and contemporary in feel and in summer the glass doors can be opened fully on to the churchyard. The terracotta, grey and yellow patterned floor of the extension was carefully chosen to match the colours of the Victorian tiles inside and the churchyard brick wall.

The Building Project Team was led by established local residents David Greasby and Tony Lascelles, a farmer and a former businessman respectively, both of whom were keen to ensure it was genuinely a village and church project. The fund-raising committee was made up of six churchgoers and six villagers. David Greasby explains that the important factor for those involved was that 'the church is one thing but it is an historic building for everybody in the community and if there was going to be fund-raising, it had to involve the whole community, not just church people, or the project would have foundered right at the start'.

The committee ran a well coordinated local fund-raising campaign and, when it came to soliciting pledges, each member focused on their road or area and wrote individually to those they knew. They also ran community events such as Midsummer Balls, Safari Suppers and a Village Open Gardens Day. There were successful sponsored walks, teddy bear drops, pub quizzes, bridge drives and art sales. In total the project cost about £175,000. A third of the money came from the village, including £5,000 jointly from the Village Community Association and the Parish Council, which proved a positive factor when they were applying for grants.

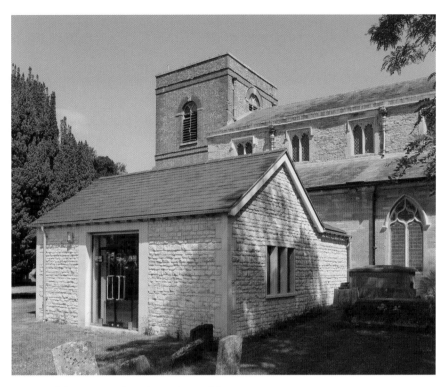

Exterior of the extension from the south-east, July 2013. PHOTO JW

Cut-away perspective showing the extension and the link to the south door, 2013.
PHOTO WALLINGFORD ARCHITECTURE LTD

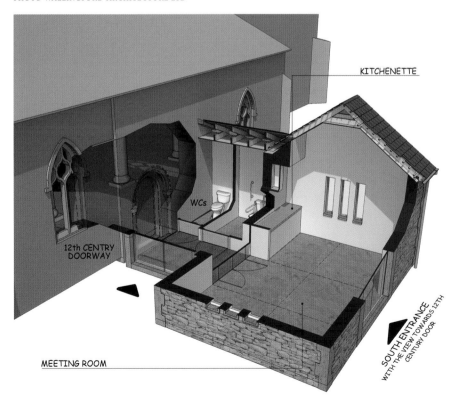

Jeremy Goulston stresses that it was very much a team project, involving both church and village people. 'It could not have been achieved without the work of the Project Team through the various stages. My role was to keep the vision alive and keep the energy going at the same time as the other calls on our time and our commitments as a worshipping community. We could not have estimated in advance the amount of commitment required by the community and the church to work together!'

The PCC is very pleased with the new Church Room and reports that it is warm and well insulated. The members now hold all their meetings in the extension 'simply because it's the right size and is far more economical than trying to heat the whole church, which we tried to do previously but failed at dismally'. The Sunday School, which used to meet in the village hall, can now meet in the extension just next to those worshipping in the main building.

A lettings committee has been formed to develop a marketing policy for the extension, which complements the village hall. The hall is mostly fully booked on weekdays and evenings, and is larger and not as suitable for groups to meet. The Summer Concert and reading and drama events will benefit from being able to use the extension rather than a marquee. The PCC wants to organise more concerts and also promote it as a place for quiet days.

Mr Goulston knows that for a project to work, goodwill is essential between church and village, and that can only be built up over time. He says, 'Villages have long memories and we have to make good cases for what we are doing and understand for ourselves why we are doing it and what we are about.' Showing what the church can offer the community is key. In Brightwell, well-known church people have been contributing to the development of the Community Plans and the Community Association over the years. One of the current churchwardens is the volunteer deputy manager of the village shop, and this has strengthened links, especially when the community shop had to raise £200,000 just before St Agatha's embarked on its fund-raising campaign. Continuing the close link between village and church, the Steering Group of the 2014 Community Plan now meets in the extension and several church people also serve on the various subcommittees.

CHALLENGES

One of the big problems was keeping the cost down. It is vital to prepare a detailed budget, obtain full estimates for all elements of the project and keep control of the budget so that you always know where the money is being spent. There is a high level of financial responsibility involved when you are working with public and local residents' money.

LESSONS LEARNED

It is essential to separate responsibility for detailed project management from responsibility for fund-raising. People need to be able to concentrate on their own areas, but ensure that communication between the two is regular and open.

Talk to grant people early to understand their process and conditions, even if they are not necessarily going to give you a grant. In this case, a grant of £20,000 from the Rural Development Programme for England proved the most difficult to obtain and came with the highest number of conditions. It was also nearly lost, as there was no allowance for extensions of the claim period.

BEST PIECE OF ADVICE

Running a project like this is a long haul, so ensure you have a good team around you with plenty of stamina. They need it to stay focused throughout the fund-raising campaign and to work through the various stages of submitting planning applications under both the ecclesiastical and planning systems.

A business plan is essential to satisfy the grant-making bodies as well as the DAC, and it ensures that you have thought through all aspects of your project.

WEBSITE

St Agatha's is fully integrated within the Brightwell-cum-Sotwell website: http://www.brightwellcumsotwell.co.uk/ pwpcontrol.php?pwpID=5536

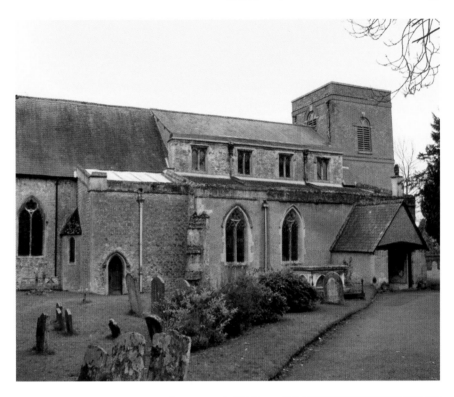

Above Exterior from the north, November 2004. PHOTO JW

Right Interior showing servery, looking through the glass door into the link and the twelfth-century door into the church, July 2013. Toilets on right. PHOTO JW

Below Extension from the west showing the link with the church, July 2013. PHOTO BP

Below right The extension in use during a concert, June 2013. PHOTO RICHARD MASON

St John the Baptist, Burford

The project will not happen unless God is behind it. We need to trust that the Lord will continue to lead in his timing and will provide all of the resources required. We will succeed through prayer, hard work and by continuing to move forward in faith.

Ian Brown, churchwarden 2004–2013

Burford, 'The Gateway to the Cotswolds', is an historic town of 1,300 inhabitants on the River Windrush in West Oxfordshire. The Grade 1 listed church is just behind the main street.

The building dates from around 1175. It benefited from the generosity of successive generations of fleece and wool merchants, who, in a reflection of their wealth and civic pride, added the transepts, a Guild Chapel and several other chapels. The prominent tower and spire were built in 1495 and later the Guild Chapel was incorporated into the church and dedicated as the Lady Chapel. It was heavily restored and reordered by G. E. Street in the 1870s and 1880s.

Warwick Hall is listed Grade 11 and dates from the mid-nineteenth century. It was at one point used as part of the church school and is situated just outside the churchyard south gates.

THE PROJECT

A £3.3 million redevelopment of Warwick Hall. The aim is to create a multi-purpose building that will provide space for a wide range of church and community groups to meet, facilities for catering, office space, rooms for performance and seminars as well as space for fellowship and prayer.

As well as adapting and refurbishing Warwick Hall, the plan is to construct a second hall to the east with a seating capacity of 200.

The halls will be linked by a central two-storey building housing meeting rooms and all the ancillary functions such as toilets and kitchens as well as the foyer and café. A new entrance to the north side of the link building from within the churchyard will be created. This is seen as critical to achieving new level access throughout and providing a stronger link between the church and the new complex.

REALISATION

Over the last ten years, the PCC has undertaken a major repairs programme including work on the roof and the interior fabric. In 2004, a major reordering of the church was undertaken with the guidance of Acanthus Clews Architects, and the existing wooden chairs were replaced with more comfortable ones. The pews had been removed in three stages from the 1970s to the late 1990s. The heating system was upgraded and a new flexible lighting scheme was designed and installed. In 2006 the west door was modified to allow disabled access. A portable dais is now used, improving visibility in a church with a very long chancel and distant high altar.

A servery with a large, fully fitted kitchen has been discreetly installed at the west end of the Lady Chapel and there is a fully accessible toilet at the east end of the south aisle.

Part of the work was paid for by a very generous legacy of £350,000, part by the Friends of Burford Church and the rest by the Fabric Fund, which is funded by church giving.

The seating arrangements can now be changed for different services and events. Although the seats normally face east, the PCC has experimented with facing them west or north during more informal services. Concerts, dances, banquets and lunches have also been held in the church.

Included in Simon Jenkins's *England's Thousand Best Churches* and awarded five stars, the church

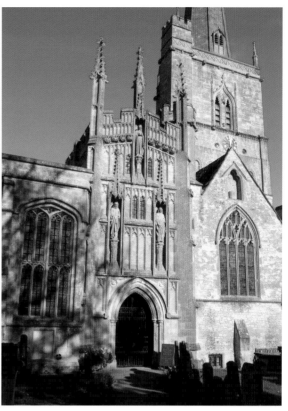

Right View of south porch entrance, June 2009.
PHOTO DAVE STEWART, ACANTHUS CLEWS ARCHITECTS

Above Interior looking east with the earlier wooden chairs, May 2003. PHOTO JW

Below Looking across the nave towards the east end with the new chairs and lighting system in place, November 2006.
PHOTO DAVE STEWART, ACANTHUS CLEWS ARCHITECTS

receives 50,000 visitors a year. It caters for this by employing a part-time verger and using volunteers to welcome the visitors, and by providing a guidebook in a number of languages. In 2007 new wrought-iron and glazed doors were installed at the south porch for security and to reduce draughts. This also enables the porch to be used as a welcoming area.

The PCC is now creating a quiet prayer area in the north transept. Ian Brown says that because the church receives so many visitors, some on tours, 'it doesn't work always for those wanting to find a quiet space'. The quiet area will also offer space for parents with young children during services. The current prayer space is in the Chapel of St Thomas, adjacent to the south porch, which is accessible only by a flight of steps. Agreement could not be reached on installing a stair lift so the PCC has been involved in discussions with English Heritage and the DAC on how best to enclose the north transept in order to provide a soundproof space, while not blocking sightlines and ensuring it is still possible to walk around the church. The final proposal is to fill in the three open arches with glass within a wooden frame and to put doors in two sides. In November 2013 the Friends of Burford Church voted to spend the required £50,000 to make it happen.

The PCC feels the church works well as a place of worship, and as a visitor destination, but that there is limited potential to develop the building further to provide the space for its youth and children's work. Ian Brown says that 'it is a challenge all the time between being a glorious historic church and trying to contain our ever-growing congregation'. At one point, the PCC wanted to make the 'more accessible' west door the main entrance and build a new glass lobby to make it more user-friendly. But it has been advised that this would not be given approval by the DAC.

Warwick Hall is on the south edge of the churchyard boundary and has been accommodating numerous community and church groups over the last fifty years or so. It is owned by St John the Baptist's, but had been leased to the Town Council on a thirty-year lease that expired in April 2012. The PCC is again responsible for the property and has taken the opportunity to work with Acanthus

Clews to investigate the potential of redeveloping it. Without improvement, Warwick Hall is inadequate for present and future use by the church and community. Its size, layout and accessibility problems mean it does not meet modern standards and, crucially, it is too small for the activities that the church would like to hold there.

The 2011 Burford Community Plan, *Burford, Today and Tomorrow*, states that while Burford has a variety of alternative meeting venues, none provides a large, versatile community hall and that this shortcoming is keenly felt and restricts community activity. It agrees that although 'Warwick Hall is currently extensively used by societies and other groups, its facilities are outdated and the venue has become unattractive for most functions'.

The PCC's vision for the project is that the new facility will become the 'Heart of the Church's Ministry and the Heart of the Community's Life'. The PCC states that, although the project is being led by the church, it is committed to ensuring that the plan provides a community facility for a town that does not have one.

As with any large building project, especially one involving an historic building, many questions have been asked about its size, design and cost. The PCC emphasises that the scale of the project is driven by the need to meet both church and community requirements. 'We expect all the current users of Warwick Hall to continue using the new building, plus many additional users, because of better facilities. We expect the number of church activities to increase, especially for youth and young families,' says Ian Brown.

Some unease has been caused by the failure of previous community projects that were supported by public money but fell through. Concern was expressed about how much access the community would continue to have to the new buildings. The PCC responded by holding a two-day consultation prior to the planning application, and the plans have been displayed in the Lady Chapel over the last year. The PCC has also given presentations to Burford Town Council, provided updates for the local *Bridge* magazine and included articles in the church magazine *LogOn*. Both these publications go to every

Above Flowers for a wedding, looking towards the west end,
May 2012. PHOTO IAN BROWN

Right People looking at plans of the development of Warwick Hall
in the Lady Chapel, September 2011. PHOTO IAN BROWN

Below View of existing Warwick Hall and proposed new hall
and link building seen from the south porch of the church, April
2010. ACANTHUS CLEWS ARCHITECTS

house in the area and detailed information and the plans are on the church website.

There were several objections to the initial planning application concerning the proposed height of the new build, the design of the main entrance and the cutting down of trees in the churchyard. The PCC and the architect have worked to address all the concerns, including lowering the roof ridge, and planning permission has now been granted. The Mayor of Burford and the Town Council are now publicly behind the scheme.

Some objections remain, but a significant factor in strengthening relations with the town was an agreement with the Burford Charity Trustees to provide the premises for a community day centre for the elderly and the necessary facilities in the new hall. This has added about £200,000 to the total project cost. In March 2013 a pledge was received from the Falkland Hall Trust, which was set up with the sole purpose of providing a community hall for Burford. Warwick Hall post-redevelopment was identified as the most suitable location. The Revd Richard Coombs says that 'this pledge is wonderful in terms of commitment from the town to the project'.

Key to managing such a large project is getting the right structures in place. The PCC has had a project team in place for three years. It is currently made up of a chairman, representatives from the Design Fabrication Team, the Aesthetics Group, the Fund-Raising Team, the Clergy Team and other experienced individual members. The team meets approximately every two months, reports directly to the PCC and has been delegated responsibility for contracts and for managing the work. Three members of the Design Fabrication Team attend the monthly meetings with design consultants Acanthus Clews.

The funding strategy was to approach the church community first and then apply for grants. There is a large and growing congregation in Burford, many from surrounding villages. At the moment the PCC has not been very successful in obtaining grants except from local Burford charities who have been exceptionally generous, pledging £300,000. By October 2013, £1.94 million of the £3.3 million needed had been raised. The extended conceptual design phase (pre-planning approval) cost an additional £130,000 and was funded completely by one local donor.

A second pledge day within the church family was launched in October 2013 and took place on 17 November, raising an additional £660,000, taking the total at the end of November to £2.6 million. The next stage was to launch an appeal within the community and to approach local individuals who could support the project. Other fund-raising events have included a 'Strictly Burford' music night for the whole town, an auction, a Burford Church Cookbook and a dinner. Some of these are intended to raise large amounts of money, others are to make sure that the whole community feels involved and part of the project.

The current timetable will enable the works to begin in March 2014 and the new facility to open for use in October 2015.

CHALLENGES

The PCC has decided not to ask for Lottery funds as it has concerns about the Christian morality of such funding. This is not understood by the local community, including the Town Council, and may affect its financial contributions. The PCC is trying to find a clear way of explaining its position.

BEST PIECE OF ADVICE

For a development of this size, it is imperative that a project team is formed of people with a range of skills, including those with experience of working on commercial, non-church projects. The team should report directly to the PCC.

Consideration should be given to employing a project manager, as well as the architect, if there is no suitable expertise in the church.

Although the vicar is key to the success of a project, and probably needs to be seen as the 'leading light', he must not be overburdened by it.

WEBSITE
http://www.burfordchurch.org/

St Nicholas, Chadlington

Even though it revealed the many concerns there were about making any changes to the church, the questionnaire was very good at helping to hone down what the village wanted from the building and how we might adapt it for those purposes. The Revd Mark Abrey, Rector

Chadlington is a small village of about 800 inhabitants in the Evenlode Valley about three miles south of Chipping Norton. This rather sprawling settlement is made up of five 'ends', formerly individual hamlets in their own right: Green End, Brook End, West End, Mill End and East End, in the last of which the parish church is situated, adjacent to the manor and close to the school.

The Grade II* listed church is late twelfth-century with thirteenth- and fifteenth-century additions. In 1870 it was restored and the chancel rebuilt by Charles Buckeridge with the addition, on the south side, of a vestry and organ chamber with a crypt (boiler room) below.

THE PROJECT

Between August 2007 and April 2008 the church was closed for reordering. Mains water, gas and drainage were brought in. The crypt was refurbished for a new boiler, servicing a new central heating system with wall-mounted radiators and partial underfloor heating in the nave, which was refloored with York stone. The building was rewired throughout and new lighting and a sound system installed.

A fully accessible toilet was installed in the west tower vestry beneath a new floor reached by a staircase. An oak servery was constructed against the west wall of the south aisle. More than half the original wooden pews were removed from the west end of the nave and both aisles, creating a gathering space for post-service refreshments and community functions. A dedicated children's area and meeting room was created in the north transept. The long-disused north door was reopened. Finally, cleaning and redecorating the interior created a light and airy building.

REALISATION

Towards the end of the 1990s, the PCC began to feel that the church was no longer meeting the needs of the parishioners, and wanted to make it more welcoming and accessible by providing the flexibility to host a variety of functions. Specifically, the aim was to find ways to increase regular family involvement. However, it was after the Revd Mark Abrey arrived in 2001 that the project began to gain momentum. He says, 'In the beginning there was considerable opposition to any of the proposed changes from within the PCC, the wider congregation and the parish as a whole. For a time it seemed that it was only a minority view that something needed to be done if the church was to survive as a thriving entity.' The key to progress had to be listening to and addressing the concerns of the majority, ensuring that there was open discussion about every step and giving an undertaking that nothing would be bulldozed through in the face of opposition.

In April 2002 the PCC sent out a description of the proposals, together with a detailed questionnaire, to the whole parish. Respondents were asked if they were in favour of developing the use of the building for community activities and if they were in favour, against, unsure or undecided about each of the proposals. In all, 450 questionnaires were delivered and 246 replies were received – a 55% response. The replies were collated and a detailed report was produced in July which recorded the 'yes' and 'no' responses graphically. Written comments for each question were recorded verbatim, those of regular church members differentiated throughout from those of the wider parish.

The responses showed that there was some opposition to all the proposals; some from church members but most from the wider community. This was particularly so where the questionnaire listed specific areas, such as the addition of a kitchen and facilities, the possible relocation of the organ, the replacement of the pipe organ with an electronic instrument, screening the north transept and using the church for drama. The biggest recorded 'no' was over the proposal to remove the pews to provide a more flexible seating system. Many saw the pews as essential to the traditional spiritual feel of the church and there was general anxiety over losing the special atmosphere of the building (despite the fact that it was dark, cold and in urgent need of redecoration). Among the concerns expressed were the huge 'unnecessary' cost of introducing new features, and, as one person put it, trying to turn the church into an 'entertainment centre and café'. Another thought was that the nearby Memorial Hall, refurbished for the millennium, should be used to provide these facilities. There were also many supportive responses and suggestions.

These responses helped to narrow down what the project should be about, and enabled the PCC to respond sensitively to the concerns, as well as to take on board the positive suggestions made. A planning subcommittee of the PCC was established to consider the options and to report back to the full committee; at the same time a fund-raising subcommittee was formed. Both subcommittees contained co-opted members with expertise in their specific field. An early idea, mooted by a visiting expert in church reordering, was to use architectural glass to infill the north and south arcades, creating separate zones of activity with independent heating and lighting. Apart from the obvious cost implications, it was considered that the church was too small and the sense of spaciousness and the full impact of the historic architecture could be lost. The planning subcommittee therefore concentrated on identifying which activities the church should be able to host,

what new facilities would be needed to service them, and where these facilities should be located.

Acanthus Clews Architects were appointed in 2003 to develop a scheme. This was presented to the parish at an open meeting to ensure that all who were interested could be involved and to show that their comments had been taken on board. The tower vestry was identified as the optimum location for the toilet, behind an oak screen and door, providing the necessary privacy and separation from the main body of the church. To make better use of the space between the vestry and the ringing chamber, a mezzanine floor was constructed to provide a small meeting room, accessed by a new staircase. Unfortunately, changes to Health and Safety legislation, introduced during the construction work, decreed that the new space could not be used as intended, as the stairs were too steep. However, the new room became a useful concealed store for some of the folding chairs later purchased. As part of this work, the fluted glass window above the tower vestry screen was replaced with clear glass, restoring an attractive view of the west window.

Insufficient space remained in the tower vestry for a servery, so this was constructed in English oak against the west wall in the south aisle. When not in use it appears as a discreet row of cupboards but sections of the top lift up to reveal a sink, taps and work surfaces, while the left-hand end conceals a movable service trolley with crockery storage.

Locating these facilities at the west end of the church suggested that, logically, this was the obvious area for the planned new activities; but this was the most difficult issue that the PCC had to deal with. At an early planning stage it had been proposed that all the existing pews should be removed and replaced by chairs, but this was rejected by a large majority of those who responded to the questionnaire. Thus the plan was for all the pews to be retained apart from those in the north transept. Then, as Mr Abrey explained, 'All the pews were moved out of the church while the stone floor and new heating system were installed. Two members of the PCC who had been most adamant that the pews must be retained came to see me and said that, actually, the space looks so beautiful, can we just put back six pews each

Above Exterior from the south, March 2007. PHOTO JW

Top left Before works done, looking from the south aisle across to the north transept, October 2003. PHOTO REVD MARK ABREY

Centre left Interior before works done, showing all pews in place and carpets, March 2007. PHOTO JW

Bottom left After works done, looking from south aisle towards meeting room in north transept, July 2013. PHOTO BP

Below 'Messy Church' in the meeting room with the screens folded back, 2013. PHOTO REVD MARK ABREY

side of the centre of the nave?' This was agreed, and the twelve pews, now no longer fixed to the floor, can seat some seventy members of the congregation, more than sufficient for a normal Sunday service. For larger services such as weddings and funerals, for concerts or other special events, additional seating is easily provided by the new folding chairs. As the remaining pews, which are wooden benches with open backs, are relatively light and now movable, it is possible to host such events as, for example, the Maundy Thursday supper, when they can be moved to the side and replaced by tables down the whole length of the nave.

The original plan to replace the existing quarry-tiled and wooden floor in the nave with York stone paving was rejected by the PCC on cost grounds. An alternative plan was devised to reuse the existing floor, with the tiles and boards relaid after the installation of the underfloor heating, the wood being sanded and sealed. However, when the old floor was lifted it became obvious that many of the supporting joists were rotten and would need replacing. This unforeseen additional expenditure rendered the cost of the stone floor feasible and the PCC voted to reintroduce that option. The stone floor works well with the underfloor heating and together with the redecoration has brought a uniform look to the nave and aisles.

The children's area and meeting room was created in the north transept by infilling the arches with oak-framed architectural glass above oak folding screens, allowing the space to become a separate room or part of the main body of the church for larger events. The aim was to create a space for community use, particularly by the neighbouring church school. Initially it was used at least once a week by different classes for more reflective lessons, including Godly Play. Disappointingly, however, it has not been used as regularly during the last two years as the PCC hoped. Although there is not currently a Sunday School, it is used by parents with smaller children with the screens open so that they can still be involved in the service.

The total cost of the project was £252,500. To ensure that the normal church finances were unaffected, a separate Development Fund account

was opened by the PCC in November 2003 when fund-raising started, and functioned until February 2012. Of the total raised, over £42,000 came from various trusts, including the Oxfordshire Historic Churches Trust, and a further £20,000 was secured from the (European-funded) Leader Plus Fund, administered by West Oxfordshire District Council, specifically for the meeting room. Almost £114,000 was raised through donations from the congregation and parishioners; this included two individual gifts of £15,000 in response to an emergency appeal to cover the unbudgeted additional cost of the stone flooring. There were numerous fund-raising events, among them three concerts by a visiting Russian choir and three by the Choral Scholars of King's College, Cambridge. There was a series of very successful Face to Face evenings at which famous figures were interviewed by other well-known people: among the subjects were author Philip Pullman and David Cameron (twice – before he became Prime Minister), interviewed by the diplomat Peter Jay and again by Jane Moore, then of the *Sun*. There were cheese and wine tastings, Open Garden days, an Auction of Promises and ferret racing, among other events. Mr Abrey says that these events had the added bonus of bringing the community together. 'There was a buzz about the place and the PCC has said we have got to keep doing this sort of thing because it is really positive.'

The PCC feels that the changes have respected the integrity of the building, while enhancing it aesthetically, and have created a space which is much more conducive to worship and other activities. The church is warm, light and airy and there is real flexibility in the ways the available space can be used. Every two months, on a Sunday afternoon, children and their parents come to 'Messy Church', when tables are put up and craft activities and games with a religious theme take place.

There is a feeling that the local community now has a sense of ownership of the building; it is seen as a very good place for concerts and is an important venue for the Dean and Chadlington Music Festival, held each June. It is used weekly for rehearsals by a community choir. Music in the church has been enhanced by the acquisition of an excellent grand piano, made possible by the additional space, on permanent loan from a generous parishioner. For the last four years the church has hosted an art exhibition as part of the Oxfordshire Arts Week, and has accommodated the PCC's annual Christmas Fayre, formerly held in the Memorial Hall.

While the church does attract many visitors and has, on occasion, raised over £700 in a week from coffees and teas, the PCC is currently exploring ways of encouraging more use of the room in the north transept. Discussions with the school are considering the possibility of resuming regular pupil visits. In a relatively small village with other facilities including the Memorial Hall, a popular sports and social club, a bowls club and a café, the building's full potential has still to be achieved.

CHALLENGE

The main demand on everyone involved was probably the sheer time and effort spent in managing and successfully completing such a project; the overall control was in the hands of the incumbent and the Standing Committee of the PCC.

WEBSITE

The church has a weekly bulletin downloadable from http://www.achurchnearyou.com/chadlington-st-nicholas/

Top Looking across the west end showing the new servery in the south aisle, toilets at base of tower, retained pews and new folding chairs, July 2013. PHOTO BP

Centre View from within the meeting room, July 2013. PHOTO BP

Bottom Looking down the north aisle towards the meeting room in the north transept, July 2013. PHOTO BP

St Mary the Virgin, Chalgrove

The challenge in terms of reordering and modernising has been to bring a traditional church up to date without losing its special character. It is important not to have a set view of what a church should look like. The Revd Canon Ian Cohen

Chalgrove is a large rural village in South Oxfordshire with a population of about 3,500. Several new housing estates built since the 1970s, alongside the older thatched cottages, mean that the village can support six shops, including a post office, and three pubs. It is noted for the Chalgrove Brook running the length of the High Street and for being the site of the Civil War Battle of Chalgrove Field, during which Parliamentarian John Hampden was fatally wounded.

St Mary the Virgin is a Grade 1 listed building dating from the twelfth century. Although subsequently altered it is thought to remain substantially as it was in 1500, with only minor alterations in the eighteenth century. It has a wide nave with two aisles separated by transitional Norman arcades with carved capitals and a chancel.

The chancel contains a nearly complete set of nationally important medieval wall paintings dedicated to St Mary the Virgin. It is believed that they were painted around 1320, probably at the behest of the de Barantyn family, who lived in one of the two manors in Chalgrove. They were lime-washed over in the Reformation and rediscovered in 1858 during renovations.

THE PROJECT

In 2007 a servery and two toilets, one fully accessible, were installed at the base of the west tower, providing a new floor to the ringing chamber above. A new spiral staircase was designed for the new bell chamber. Cupboard space has been provided for flower arrangers' requirements. This is all hidden behind an existing Victorian wooden screen. A small viewing window was installed above the screen so that the bell-ringers can see down the nave. The pews have been movable for over twenty-five years, and have been retained.

REALISATION

This is a case where several buildings – the two churches of St Mary and St Helen, another community building, as well as three cottages and a pub – have over the past twenty-five years been gradually renovated and modernised so that each in different ways is offering a service or facility to the local community.

For Canon Cohen, 'the aim of the church is to mark the important stages in people's lives such as marriage and death and to be involved in every part of their lives. We are a church that believes that God wants us to be welcoming and hospitable, serving and building within our community, and that is what we are trying to do.'

When Ian Cohen first arrived in 1988, he felt firmly that the first thing to be achieved was the renovation and modernisation of the Red Lion pub and the three cottages vested in the Trustees of the Church Estate. All were in a neglected state. He and the Trustees worked to ensure they are all now rented out and that the pub is operating as a viable business. This was to illustrate that the church was concerned about buildings that mattered to the community, that it could be trusted, and was being a responsible landlord.

The Church Estate also had to be made to run efficiently. After running and maintenance costs, the remaining income can support the renovation of the

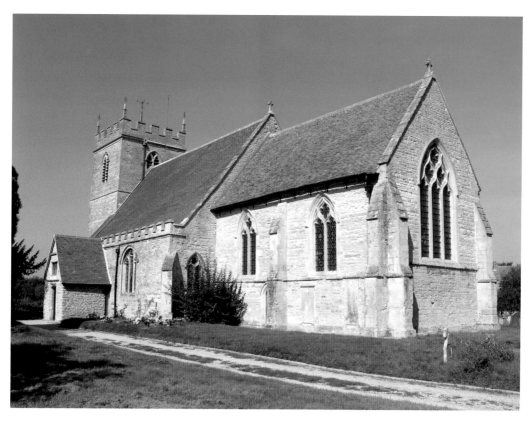

Exterior from the south-east, September 2004. PHOTO JW

Looking towards the east end showing angled pews, June 2013. PHOTO BP

church's fabric and other aspects of its services.

In 2000, the John Hampden Hall, the church hall, was refurbished to provide small offices and meeting rooms. It is run by the John Hampden Trust, made up of volunteers separate from the PCC, although many are members of St Mary's. It continues to be a facility for the whole community; it is available for hire and manages to pay for itself. This was to show locals what the church was doing for the community before works to the actual church interior started.

Canon Cohen is very clear that the aim is to work together, not in competition, with other community facilities. Chalgrove can support its community buildings and especially the village hall, the church hall and the church itself. They are different in scale and type and complement each other. The village hall is big enough for very large gatherings, while the John Hampden Hall is good for private parties and small groups and is located in the centre of the village. The church can offer the best acoustics and less time pressure. During Oxford Arts Week, even very large pieces of artwork could stay up for the whole eight days and did not have to be taken down for regular functions.

The other church in the benefice is the much smaller Grade II* listed St Helen's, Berrick Salome. Its glory is its very fine seventeenth-century oak timber roof and gallery and oak-panelled fixed box pews. Found at the end of a long and winding road, the church is very popular for weddings and concerts and there are no plans to do anything that will change its special, intimate atmosphere. There is a congregation of between seven and twenty-four every Sunday and they manage to pay their parish share.

When it came to St Mary's, the first priority was to ensure that the fabric of the building was in good repair. There was serious damp to be dealt with and in 2003 further repair works were carried out, culminating in re-roofing in 2005.

Inside, the church is very light, partly because of the white walls and columns and partly because there is very little stained glass, as most of it was destroyed during the Civil War. The PCC started by restoring the important historic artefacts inside. The chancel wall paintings were inspected and cleaned. The 1840s Chalgrove Friendly Society banner was restored and

the turret clock, dating back to around 1699 and thought to be one of the oldest working clocks in Oxfordshire, was fully restored.

The PCC then organised the listing and prioritising of what needed to be done to update the church and encourage more use of it by the wider community. Main priorities were agreed to be a new bell chamber and the need for facilities within the church. Because there was an existing, if old, heating system, toilets were assigned a higher priority as an essential factor in encouraging more activities, rather than having 'a sort of embarrassing loo tent hidden somewhere in the churchyard'.

With architect Patrick Crawford of Caroe and Partners it was decided to locate the facilities at the base of the west tower underneath the new bell chamber. This would not alter the worshipping atmosphere but would retain the overall unity of the rest of the space. Inserting a mezzanine floor into the space without a major intrusion into the medieval arch created a challenge and, in the end, the floor was supported on steel pillars. Several options were considered for the new chamber, including the design and position of the new staircase, and there had to be enough room to work all six bell-ropes. The chamber was designed to be totally reversible and remains hidden behind an existing Victorian pine screen. This work cost £186,000, of which about £35,000 came from the community and the rest from grants.

The pine pews, which were fairly heavy, were already movable. Two pew skates or trolleys, specially designed by a member of the congregation, an engineer, were supplied to make it easier and safer to move them for a church or village event. The pews, though not remarkable, reflect the values of this church. Twenty years ago, some were in a poor state and had rotted at the ends. These rotten ends were repaired, and remain a precious asset for mission.

'One of the first things that showed what could happen was a big floral clock made as part of a flower festival, which, because the pews could be moved, could be placed right in the centre of the church, and people loved it,' said Canon Cohen.

Basically, the worship space has remained unchanged. The congregation still uses the high altar and the chancel with its magnificent fourteenth-

A pew being moved on one of the specially
designed trolleys, July 2013.

The new facilities at the base of the tower, June 2013. PHOTO BP

century wall paintings for worship. Pews are still
very important for the life of the church. 'They need
to be flexibly used, but if you have got weddings
and funerals, people want to sit on pews and feel
close to each other. If you put people in chairs they
are automatically split off from each other.' Now
that they are movable, it has been possible to place
the pews at an angle so that everyone can see more
easily. 'There is now a sense of being "in the round"
which has enhanced the worship,' says Canon Cohen.

The facilities and the flexibility of the pews
have increased the number and type of community
activities. All the pews can be moved outside
and protected under a tarpaulin for events such
as banquets, barn dances, and Parties-in-the-Pews
complete with bouncy castle. A few pews can be
taken out at the front if there is an especially large
choir or a stage is needed for theatrical productions.

The PCC is now considering a further major phase
of works focusing on the nave and chancel. This
is probably going to cost £500,000. Its members
have spent time visiting other churches, learning
from what others have achieved. Technical research
is being done on new systems and materials. This

major conservation and refurbishment project will
improve community space and facilities as well as
ensuring that the precious heritage of this church is
both preserved and better interpreted. Fund-raising
has already begun and an application to the Heritage
Lottery Fund is in progress.

Charles Baker, project manager for the whole ten
years (so far), says that they have deliberately phased
the project, as it has been important to gradually
build up trust that the PCC is looking after the church
responsibly. Its members consulted over the toilets
and the facilities at the back because they knew that
would affect people and they had to show that they
would be used and were meeting a need. Local people,
specific organisations and the school, were invited to
an Open Day, when they were shown plans of the
proposals and asked to complete a short questionnaire.
One question was 'When we have done this work,
will you make more use of the church?' There was a
very positive response which can be used to support
further grant applications.

However, the PCC has done much more
consulting on this next phase because it will affect
the worshipping space. The architect has been asked

to produce some line drawings to show what it will look like. The aim is to show that it will still be very recognisable as the church, as fears have been expressed that it was in danger of becoming too like a village hall.

The church is now used four or five times a month, which is considerably more than before. The last Chalgrove Parish Plan was completed in 2010 and the churches inserted one question: 'Do you place some value on these places of worship and if so what for?' Among the answers were funerals, weddings, the graveyard, a worship space, a quiet place for prayer, and a heritage building. Overall, 800 people responded positively to that question.

CHALLENGES
Spending enough time to solve the technical challenges arising from the insertion of the mezzanine floor.

LESSONS LEARNED
Ensure that you are included in the Community Plan. It will raise the profile of the church and mean that it is counted as a community facility. It will provide evidence to support your case for grant applications.

BEST PIECES OF ADVICE
Try to keep the development of the actual work with the architect and the DAC and the planning processes in parallel with the fund-raising. The initial fund-raising will be based on rough estimates, but you need to allow enough time to develop a strategy that will include researching and making grant applications as well as planning your own local fund-raising activities.

Speak to the DAC early on as they will provide good advice which may well save you a lot of time.

WEBSITE
http://www.chalgrovechurch.org/

Top The Victorian screen in front of the new room at the base of the tower showing the bell-ringers' viewing window and the organ, June 2013. PHOTO BP

Above A concert by 'Twelve Times a Lady' in the church, March 2013. PHOTO DR ZACHARY K. MARSHALL

St Mary the Virgin, Charlbury

We had inherited a church that the Revd Martin Chadwick, the then incumbent, described as 'a loose association of spaces'; it was a load of boxes really. And none of them properly connected with the others. Mike Summers, current churchwarden

Charlbury is a small, picturesque Cotswold town of about 3,000 people in the Evenlode Valley in West Oxfordshire. Being close to the Oxfordshire Way, it receives many visitors.

The Grade 1 listed church of St Mary the Virgin was built in the twelfth century when it belonged to Eynsham Abbey. It was enlarged in the thirteenth century, when the chancel was extended eastwards and the south aisle, west tower and north and south chapels were added. Further additions were made in the thirteenth to sixteenth centuries. In 1856, the architect G. E. Street removed the eighteenth-century galleries and refitted the church with new pine pews, and in 1874 the chancel was rebuilt by another Gothic Revival architect, Charles Buckeridge.

THE PROJECT

Between 1987 and 1995, the church underwent what is believed to be the most comprehensive restoration in its 900-year history. Essential repairs and renewals were combined with adapting the church for contemporary needs.

The old pipe organ was replaced in 1987 by an electronic organ and the empty organ chamber was transformed into a vestry, kitchen and toilet, with a meeting room above. The fabric was extensively repaired and a stone floor was laid in the nave, north and south aisles and in the Memorial Chapel. New heating and lighting as well as a sound amplifying system (with loop) were installed. A glass screen was placed around the Memorial Chapel (formerly the Pudlicote aisle) and soundproofed so that it could be used by the Sunday School during services. Most radically, especially at this time, the pews were replaced by chairs and the sanctuary and the main altar were moved to the west end.

REALISATION

As soon as you enter the church through the glass doors, something strikes you as different. You then notice that all the chairs are facing west, with their backs to the chancel. Mike Summers, the churchwarden, says that so many visitors ask about this that they have devised an explanation on their website, which forms the basis for this case study.

The PCC had already undertaken the 1987 changes mentioned above. Still to be tackled were the serious levels of dry rot, wet rot and death-watch beetle reported in the quinquennial inspections of 1985 and 1990. The wooden floor was rotten and becoming unsafe and investigation revealed that this was because the bearers supporting it had been laid directly on the bare earth.

The congregation still faced the conventional way (see plan, overleaf), which was presenting several problems. Only those in the central nave could tell what was going on. People behind pillars, in the choir stalls and the aisle couldn't see or hear anything. To mitigate this, the church had taken to having services in the Pudlicote aisle, which could accommodate more than the nave, but it was having to use the south and central aisles every Sunday for overflow from the family communion service. The Sunday School used the north aisle, but was separated from the main church only by a flimsy net curtain, and the inevitable noise disturbed the overflow congregation, who were having enough trouble following the service as it was.

The pews had to come out so that the rotten floor could be replaced, and this provided an opportunity to look at what might be a better configuration for a growing church. The poor-quality 1850s pine pews were described by one member of the congregation as presenting 'an unbroken vista of a toffee-brown sea covering the floor'. The congregation had also grown used to the chairs in the Pudlicote aisle, which were much more comfortable.

Guided by the previous incumbent, the Revd Martin Chadwick, the PCC, churchwarden Tony Leeming and architect Alan Bristow visited other churches within a radius of sixty miles for inspiration and looked at various options. The final scheme involved moving the sanctuary to the west end just in front of the base of the tower (see plan, far right).

This everyone agreed was the layout that enabled the greatest number of people to see and participate in the service. The chancel and east altar are retained for smaller, more intimate services and the Pudlicote aisle, renamed the Memorial Chapel (because the war memorial is there), has been glassed in and soundproofed to provide somewhere for the Sunday School to meet before the children rejoin their parents for communion. The floor was replaced by a Cotswold stone floor and, after much discussion, the pews were replaced by upholstered chairs, similar to those in the Pudlicote aisle.

There was some opposition to the proposal to 'face the wrong way'. It was explained that there were other examples of this, among them Coventry Cathedral. There were also objections to removing the pews. The PCC even went as far as having a mock-up made of a small pew which could be moved about, and was tried out. In the end the chairs prevailed. One member of the congregation commented that 'the beauty of the chairs is that they have got legs which you can see through to the floor, which gives much more of a sense of space and openness'. There was a tricky period when rumours flew that the church wanted to get rid of the war memorial and dig up all the gravestones, and a petition was started. The PCC worked hard to explain what it was actually planning and why.

The alterations took place between 1992 and 1995.

For about six months, services were held in the hall of the old primary school.

The total cost was £385,000, of which £280,000 came directly from parishioners. With a few small grants, the remainder was raised by intensive fund-raising events sponsored by the PCC and individual church members, by selling specially designed goods, selling the old pews and other redundant items and by donations from outside benefactors. Sunday afternoon teas raised about £150–£200 a week, more when local gardens were opened or art events were organised.

The St Mary's Kneeler Project, which ran between 1994 and 2000, was key in breaking down barriers between church and community. A matching set of kneelers now hangs on the back of every sponsored chair, designed and stitched individually by parishioners and representing symbols of the Christian faith and Church life, but also organisations and businesses within the town: Worth's Motor Services is represented by a classic car and the local hairdresser's by a crossed comb and scissors.

On entering St Mary's, the visitor is struck by the reversed arrangement. Facing the west end altar, the eye is drawn to the wooden spiral staircase leading up to the bell chamber in the tower. However, it has been a success.

The congregation now appreciates the open, lighter, generally inclusive feel in the church. The changes have revealed much more clearly the two arcades of pillars. Mike Summers says, 'In some way, it looks both newer, but also more ancient, in that you can now see the bases of the pillars against a stone floor.'

The Revd Jan Fielden, associate priest, explains, 'It's much, much better for worship as the chairs are arranged in a semicircle and everyone can see and everyone's involved.' There are now only about eight seats with limited visibility.

This is a vibrant church, with a large congregation. It is well used for activities such as Holy Week events. A Bible Study Week offers activities and story sessions for all ages and embraces the local school. There isn't as much community use as in some other churches, partly because Charlbury is well served with halls, but the church takes part in the annual

Interior before the reordering looking towards the west end, showing the choir stalls. PHOTO © CHARLBURY CHURCH

Exterior from the east, May 2013. PHOTO BP

Below Plans by Alan Bristow showing layout of church before (left) and after reordering (right), 1995

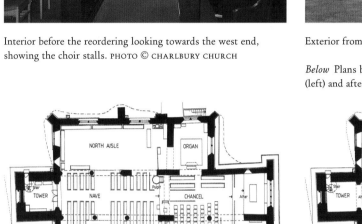

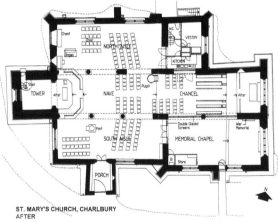

Arts Week and hosts concerts. The new organ and the raised area around the altar mean that the altar can be moved back to create a stage.

The Font Café every Thursday morning is very popular and welcomes local people to enjoy coffee and home-made cakes. Fifty or sixty people now attend, young and old, and mothers who can leave their toddlers playing safely in the Memorial Chapel. The café is helping to build new relationships between church and community.

St Mary's was presented with a special Family-Friendly Church Award by the Diocese of Oxford on 28 April 2013 in recognition of all the activities and clubs run for children and families. The church is now thinking about setting up a 'sort of faith Mother and Toddler group' for those who are interested in finding out more about the Christian faith.

The PCC is continuing to develop the church. Since the completion of the scheme in 1996, it has installed a re-glazed west window, dedicated to Martin Chadwick, the much-loved vicar under whose careful guidance the reordering was completed; provided glass doors at the south entrance (2011) to make it more welcoming; and removed the choir stalls to increase capacity in the chancel and open up the east altar.

A fire in February 2012 offered another opportunity to undertake further improvements. Ecclesiastical Insurance paid to repair the damage, but the church set up the Phoenix Fund and, reflecting

the support felt for it even among non-attenders, an additional £35,000 was raised in donations from the village. This enabled the kitchen and vestry, which were damaged by the fire and water, to be not only repaired, but updated and a wardrobe installed in the vestry for hanging vestments, all completed by November 2012. The PCC had to replace the damaged part of the vestry roof, but was able to insulate it at the same time and install a roof alarm. The sound system and audio-visual equipment have been improved and WiFi has recently been installed, which has proved popular with homeworkers.

CHALLENGES

Dealing with opposition and working with those who are unhappy with the proposals. The key is to consult. You have to carry people with you and help them feel they own the project. However brilliant a scheme is, if people haven't been given time to look at it and discuss it and ask questions, then it won't be supported.

LESSONS LEARNED

Such a big project will raise the profile of the church within the community. If people have donated to the project, they will then take an active interest.

BEST PIECE OF ADVICE

Be ready to be flexible and modify your plans if they don't provide the right solution. This may mean you have to spend a lot of time on them and reject several sets of plans.

WEBSITE

http://www.stmaryscharlbury.co.uk/

Top Facing the west end showing the new sanctuary and the pulpit, in the right foreground, May 2013. PHOTO BP

Centre Looking towards the east end chancel showing the chairs facing the new west end altar, May 2013. PHOTO BP

Bottom Bible Week activity at the west end, September 2009. PHOTO © CHARLBURY CHURCH

St Peter and St Paul, Deddington

The starting point for many of the changes that have happened since was the installation of kitchen and toilets in 1993, funded by the Parish Council.

Jim Flux, former Chair of the Parish Council

Deddington is six miles south of Banbury. With a population of about 2,200, it is a village, but with a town hall. The church, a very large one for a relatively small community, is just off the market place. Village facilities include another church, a school, a health centre and a library, mostly centrally located. The multi-purpose Windmill Community Centre on the periphery of the village offers a wide range of sports and recreational facilities.

The oldest part of the Grade II* listed church dates from the early thirteenth century. Its once tall spire collapsed on to the nave in 1634, along with the tower, rendering the building unusable for several years. Just the tower was rebuilt when the church was repaired in the mid- to late seventeenth century. The church was restored again between 1858 and 1868 by G. E. Street.

THE PROJECT

In 1993, at a cost of £38,000, a kitchen and toilets were built in a free-standing wooden unit adjacent to the south porch entrance. In 2005, a room designed by Oxford Architects was created by enclosing the area between the two pillars in the north-west corner of the church. In 2009, the pews were removed from the nave and aisles, a new floor laid and chairs introduced. In 2011, a broadband connection was put in, allowing an internet café to be set up.

REALISATION

The transformation of the church, enabling it to play a central role today in village community life, began in 1993 when the Parish Council paid the full cost of £38,000 to install four toilets, two of which are fully accessible, and a kitchen. The Parish Council had received £700,000 from the sale of land and decided that the money should be used to improve village facilities. The high interest rates of the 1990s quickly increased the sum to over £1 million. The multi-purpose Windmill Community Centre was redeveloped, a bowling green was put in and modern facilities were provided for the church. The vision of the Parish Council was that the church, the biggest and most impressive meeting place in the area as well as being in the centre of the village, should become its recognised concert hall. Concerts were already taking place there, but it had no facilities. Jim Flux, a former Chair of the Parish Council, says that 'putting in the kitchen and the toilets led people to think about what more they could do to the church'. The Revd Dr Hugh White feels that, given current trends in the reordering of churches for community use, the PCC would have raised money to put in the kitchen and toilets. The generous contribution of the Parish Council, however, meant that fund-raising efforts could be directed towards the 'more' in addition to the kitchen and toilets.

The church also benefited from the efforts of a previous incumbent, the Revd Ken Reeves, who in 1992 ran a building appeal that raised about £175,000. This fabric fund paid for subsequent repairs to the roof, windows and floor, and consequently the building has been maintained in a good state of repair.

In about 2003, the PCC took pews out at the back of the church to increase the social space for after-service coffees and post-concert refreshments.

In 2005 the area between the two pillars in the

north-west corner was enclosed and double-glazed. Named the Living Room, it was originally intended for the Sunday School and as a convenient venue for smaller meetings and services, with the advantage that the whole building does not have to be heated. It now functions as a meeting room and is used by many groups including the Boys' Brigade Company and the primary school's homework club. It houses a theological library and internet facilities, which are available to the whole village. It cost £60,500, raised by collections, one or two very generous donations and a big fund-raising programme that included sponsored jumps out of aircraft. At the same time the font was moved forward from beneath the tower into the west end of the nave, where it emphasises the importance of baptism in the life of the Church.

The PCC then experimented with placing chairs in one of the side aisles to see how people would like it, and there was surprisingly wide agreement that this worked well. So it proposed removing all the pews to create a fully flexible space for both church and community use. Recognising that the pews were of poor quality and riddled with woodworm, the DAC was happy to support the scheme. There was some opposition and it was not until 2009 that a new floor was laid and the pews were removed and sold off.

There was a big debate about what the replacement chairs should look like and how many to have. Six or seven designs were considered and, in the end, 140 solid oak chairs were purchased, including twenty with armrests for those who have difficulty getting up without extra support. The PCC purchased another 100 stackable metal and plastic chairs, kept in the aisles; this brings the seating capacity up to 250. The new floor and chairs cost £87,000. If necessary the PCC can use the additional 100 Hempton chairs that were retained, which are stored behind a new movable noticeboard.

The Parish Council has continued to be supportive. In 1998, the PCC put in floodlighting to illuminate the tower and the cost was split 50/50 between the church and the Council.

The two main community venues continue to complement each other. The Windmill Community Centre hosts about forty different clubs that use it for a variety of sporting and other activities,

while the church provides a more appropriate and aesthetically pleasing setting for concerts and drama. The Deddington Players built a wooden stage, since upgraded to a de luxe aluminium version, designed to be set up at the front of the nave when required.

The church provides the central venue for classical and jazz concerts and tribute bands, as well as some of the writing and performance events, including the community concert, that form part of the annual Deddington Festival in June, now in its eleventh year. Along with the regular craft fairs in the church, the Deddington Farmers' Market takes place on the fourth Saturday of each month in the market place, with fifteen or twenty additional stalls and refreshments inside. The church hosts the annual Village Show, an extremely popular event. The local school uses it for different activities.

Dr White believes that the church should facilitate the provision of arts within the community, as part of its central mission of witnessing to God. Managing a successful concert venue does bring practical issues, which the PCC is currently working through. There is no shortage of people wanting to hire the space, but in some months there have been several concerts in quick succession, which can result in support being spread too thin and potential attendance at each event being diminished (even though a wide range of music is offered). The PCC has set up a Church Arts Committee to try to systematise concert and arts provision by planning programmes well in advance, seeking to ensure that there are proper intervals between concerts and that clashes with other village events are avoided.

The Benefice Secretary has the responsibility of managing the bookings. There is an issue, though, says Dr White, about the need to have 'someone there on the evening making sure that the lighting and staging and other needs of the performers are in place. At the moment, this falls largely on one of the churchwardens and a few others.' The PCC is looking at how to get more people involved to provide the necessary manpower.

Currently, two charging systems operate. For some events, the performers pay a fee to the church, but take the proceeds, while for others a group will perform in return for a fee and the church takes the

Top Exterior from the south-east, June 2013. PHOTO JW

Centre Interior before works done, showing the pews, April 2006. PHOTO JW

Bottom After works done, looking towards the east end and the new chairs, July 2013. PHOTO BP

proceeds. Overall, the PCC is covering its costs. The next decision is whether it should become more pro-active and really start promoting the arts by sponsoring particular projects using the income brought in by regular events. Some PCC members are concerned about the financial risks involved, while others feel that this could be possible, but that church hire should be put on a more commercial footing first.

The PCC has continued to improve the accessibility and efficiency of the church. In 2011, a broadband connection was put in that enabled the creation of an internet café, a WiFi hotspot, a homework club for the primary school and, crucially, in 2012, the ability to broadcast both audio and video streams live from the church. It started broadcasting to a local care home and was also able to take communion to the residents during the service. Other recipients have included Radio Horton, a care home in Banbury, and iChurch.

Weddings, memorial services, Remembrance Sunday and many special events held in the church are also broadcast. The virtual congregation provided an unexpected benefit when, in November 2012, a regular visitor from Somerset tuned in to watch the All Souls Day evening service, noticed that the array of votive candles had caught fire and called the fire brigade.

The PCC has recently installed a retractable screen and projector, which has enhanced worship. There is now a film club, and lectures take place in the church.

In January 2012 a 25kW photovoltaic system was installed and has performed beyond expectation. Hidden behind the parapets, the panels are completely invisible from the ground, but a panel screen at the back of the church displays the current kW energy being generated and the resulting saving of emissions. The money for the panels came from interest-free loans and donations made by individuals, local residents as well as church members. Electricity generated provides the daytime requirements of the church while the income from selling the remainder to the National Grid is currently being used to pay back the loans. In time, this will provide additional income.

For the future, the PCC is considering redoing the kitchen and toilet block, which is looking quite shabby, is damp and rather dominates the south side of the west end of the church.

It is also investigating ways of creating a quiet space somewhere. The building's being well used, especially by the school, is a positive achievement, but it is recognised that a quiet space during the day cannot be guaranteed. Another church in the benefice is currently being considered as somewhere that could become a quiet place of pilgrimage, but this is not necessarily a solution for local Deddington people. Presently, quiet reflection is enhanced by a candle-stand and a bowl of water where you can place pebbles as a kind of prayer, at the east end of the north aisle.

CHALLENGES

Think through carefully what you may be able to offer the community. In a place with existing facilities it is important that you don't set up in competition or try to provide something that is not needed. Across a benefice some churches may be able to identify an opportunity, while others will not.

BEST PIECE OF ADVICE

As a first stage, putting in some kind of kitchen and toilets can immediately make a real difference to the usability of the building.

WEBSITE

The church website is part of the Deddington Online community website:
http://www.deddingtonchurch.org

The IT Room in the west end of the north aisle, July 2013. PHOTO BP

Toilets and kitchen block at the west end of the south aisle, July 2013. PHOTO BP

The IT Room in use, July 2013. PHOTO JUDY WARD

The Farmers' Market in the church, July 2013. PHOTOS JUDY WARD

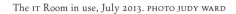

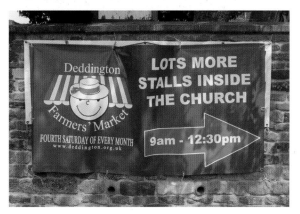

St Thomas of Canterbury, Elsfield

I think it is right that the church aspires to be the heart of the community and this was an opportunity for that to be more of a reality than just an aspiration. The Revd Tony Price

Elsfield, a very small village of about 100 inhabitants, is situated three miles north-east of Oxford, just outside the ring road. Apart from the church, which is sited on top of a hill, there are no community facilities.

The chancel and nave of this Grade II* listed church date from the late twelfth century. There was also a north aisle, possibly from this period, which was demolished. In 1849 the church was heavily restored and again in 1859, when the floor and seating were renewed under the direction of G. E. Street.

THE PROJECT

In 2002 the west end was cleared of pews to create space for the Village Room, which is separated from the nave by a specially designed folding oak and glass screen. The toilet, kitchen and storage area were housed in a new extension leading off the Village Room on the north side, where much of the earlier north aisle had been. Fabric repairs, including improved drainage and a complete rewiring, were also undertaken. New heating and lighting systems were installed.

REALISATION

This is an example of a very small congregation deciding to save its church by diversifying its uses. The work was phased systematically and, after several years of determined fund-raising involving both the church and the whole village, the building's role is secure.

In the mid-1990s, a dwindling congregation and the enormous expense of maintaining the building brought its future into question. The church was very damp and dark, with no heating, and urgent repairs had been identified. It was being used more or less only on the fifth Sunday of the month. The vicar had resigned and there was no active PCC, so a serious discussion about its viability took place at the annual Parish Meeting. Carolyn Brown, the Chair, says that there was a strong feeling that because of its heritage it could not just be closed, and that 'people have struggled through harder times than we'd had to keep it going'.

At the Parish Meeting the Archdeacon was invited to a public meeting where after a long discussion it was agreed that Elsfield should join with St Nicholas, Old Marston, and become the Parish of Marston with Elsfield, thus ensuring that services would continue to be held at St Thomas's.

The retired Dean of Christ Church, Oxford, Eric Heaton, an Elsfield resident at the time, suggested using St Thomas's as a community resource for the whole village, as there were no other public buildings. A newly formed PCC for St Thomas's decided to pursue this option.

The quinquennial architects, Carden and Godfrey, were asked to look at how a community space could be provided at the west end. Originally, they thought about putting in a mezzanine floor to create a second room above, which would have helped to keep the lower room warm. This was rejected once it was realised it would cut across the two large thirteenth-century lancet windows at the west end. The size of the extension was restricted, as it could not go beyond the west end or beyond the nineteenth-century lancet window halfway up the north nave wall. One of the buttresses was incorporated into the

Above The west end showing the recent extension housing the new facilities with the vestry annexe behind, July 2013. PHOTO BP

Top left Looking into the Village Room, July 2013. PHOTO JW

Centre left View from within the Village Room, showing the door in the north wall leading to the extension housing the facilities, July 2013. PHOTO JW

Bottom left The new signboard, July 2013. PHOTO BP

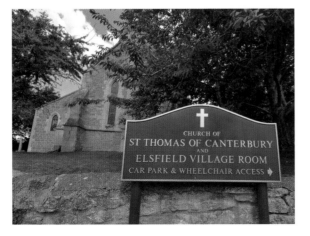

extension. Early on, it was decided a screen would ensure that people did not need to feel they were in church when they were attending a social function. The sustainability of the project depended on as many people as possible wanting to use the space.

In total the works cost about £250,000, of which about £43,000 went on repairs, an enormous sum for such a small community to raise. Included was the cost of additional works identified when the floor under the pews was found to be soaking wet and rotten. The extra costs delayed the installation of a French drain and soakaways to prevent water running into the building from the top of the hill until all the internal works had been completed. Likewise, the need to raise £8,000 to provide a ramp to improve access meant that this work was not completed for a further two years. Although the Village Room was opened in 2003, fund-raising continued until 2006.

Initially, applying for grants was dispiriting. Some trusts thought the project was worthwhile but were unconvinced that it was achievable by such a small community. The Millennium Fund seemed interested only in funding village halls and did not recognise church projects that encompassed the creation of community space. The SODC Community Trust Fund was able to give money only to a community project.

It was decided to establish a clear organisational and financial distance between the church and the community by setting up the Village Room Committee in June 2000 to complete the fund-raising and building works. The committee included both members of the church and non-churchgoing residents.

This enabled SODC to award the project a £99,000 grant, which opened the door to other grants from WREN (Waste Recycling Environmental) (£30,000), Bretts Charity, a village charity (£13,000), Oxfordshire County Council (£14,255), the Oxfordshire Historic Churches Trust (£10,000), the Oxford Preservation Trust (£10,000) and several other smaller funds. A Lottery Award for All paid for the new tables and chairs.

The driving force was Carolyn Brown, one of the two churchwardens, who kept the project going for the nearly twelve years it took. The main village fund-raising effort came from regular plant sales, which ran throughout the twelve years and raised a total of £55,000. A resident, a keen gardener, set up a 'nursery' and, with the regular help of a group of enthusiasts, plants were professionally grown. A significant contribution was made by huge bric-à-brac sales run in conjunction with the plant sales. £2,000 was made in the first year; the most successful year raised £8,000. A number of local residents gave their time to help with certain elements of the building works, such as external pointing and digging trenches in advance of the new drainage system, which gave the building a chance to dry out.

The only physical intrusion into the fabric was in the north wall of the Village Room, to create the doorway into the extension. The new build provides a fully accessible toilet, baby-changing area and storage for the tables and chairs. A short corridor leads into the fully fitted kitchen. The floor is of red and black tiles to match those that remain in the nave. The rest of the nave and chancel remains unchanged, and as it is a small church they still use the high altar. The retained pews in the nave can seat about forty, which is sufficient for the regular congregation.

At the west end, a beautiful, carefully designed and well executed space has been created. The two colours of the wooden floor mark out a cross from west to east. The architect designed a decorative balustrade above the screen that incorporates squares of coloured glass, echoing the windows at the west end. Carolyn Brown stresses: 'It has proved worth the effort to raise the extra money in order to create an elegant space.' The wardens make a point of always putting the chairs and tables away so that the church can once again become a place of peace and calm. The screen can be closed for meetings; forty people can be seated at tables, more if the screen is folded back. For larger services, more chairs can be put in place, to provide seating for a hundred people.

During the winter the night storage heating, installed as part of the project, is kept on continuously to air the building and prevent a recurrence of the damp problem. Additional overhead heaters can be switched on when the church is being used, much more efficient than turning the heating on hours beforehand.

The Village Room was formally opened by the Lord Lieutenant of Oxfordshire in 2003. The Village Room Committee, as provided for in its constitution, is responsible for its maintenance. This was necessary because of the grants awarded to a community project. Carolyn Brown says that it is also important because it allows people who may not wish to support the church to support the Village Room. 'We try and keep it separate, so for instance the Harvest Supper is organised by the Village Room Committee so that people who don't come to church don't feel uncomfortable. It encourages more people to come into the building.'

Now that the room is operational, the committee needs to raise funds for the running and maintenance costs, currently £4,000 a year. It holds events such as the Harvest Supper, the St George's Day supper, bric-à-brac sales, beetle drives, children's entertainments and Christmas fairs.

It is hired out to village residents and, at a slightly higher fee, to outsiders. For other groups, such as the Women's Fellowship, there is no charge. Carolyn Brown says, 'The only way in a small community is to play it by ear. And because we haven't any major overheads apart from electricity and maintenance, it is not difficult now to keep it going. Financially, the situation is stable with the income from letting and fund-raising.' She acknowledges that it is quite difficult to find community uses 'because in such a small community there are not regular weekly or fortnightly groups, so we are always trying to generate occasional uses for it'. It is gradually getting better known and being used by people from outside the village. The PCC has promoted it as a place for parish quiet days and other group activities.

The Village Room has made a huge difference to the community because having somewhere to hold meetings and events has helped to unite it. It has raised the profile of the church and the Revd Tony Price says there is 'more of a community ownership of the church'. There is still only one service a month, which through summer alternates between Matins and Evensong, in addition to the festivals of Christmas, Easter and Whitsun. The congregation has grown and is able to enjoy coffee after services. Income for the church has also increased through giving and fund-raising, which is important for the future maintenance of the building.

The Elsfield Parish Plan of 2009 recorded that the church is seen as key to the community and acknowledged the importance of the work of the Village Room Committee in securing continuing funding for the valuable communal space. A recommendation to the Parish Meeting stated that 'it should actively encourage residents to support the Village Room Committee's fund-raising by proposing/ participating in events'. The church notice-board facing the road proudly states 'Church of St Thomas of Canterbury and Elsfield Village Room'.

The confidence gained from its achievement has given the PCC the stamina, with the help of several grants, to raise £50,000 to restore a mosaic behind the altar which had deteriorated through damp. It depicts the Last Supper and was made in the 1860s by Salviati, the Venetian developer of 'mass-produced' methods of mosaic production.

CHALLENGES

Separating the grants awarded for repairs and other grants that were specifically for the community space was a challenge once works had started. The right pots of money to pay for the different parts of the work had to be identified as each bill arrived.

LESSONS LEARNED

The architects were brilliant, but based in London. There are advantages to using a local architect who is more able to make short visits to sort out immediate problems.

BEST PIECE OF ADVICE

Bear in mind there will be ongoing costs, not just the initial sum. After raising the money to set something up, it is hard work to continue to raise enough to keep it going.

WEBSITE

http://www.godspell.org.uk/nicholas/elsfield.shtml

Looking from the chancel down to the west end, July 2013.
PHOTO BP

St John the Evangelist, Fernham

We have not only provided a building for the community, which needed one, but provided a mechanism by which the church building, which remains a place of worship, is managed and supported by the community, and that is a really significant development. Neil Sutherland, former Chair of Project Inspire

Fernham is a small village with a population of about 250, two miles south of Faringdon in the Vale of White Horse district. The small Grade II listed church, on an elevated site at the centre of the village, was built in 1861 in thirteenth-century style by the Gothic Revival architect J. W. Hugall as a chapel of ease for the neighbouring village of Longcot.

THE PROJECT

A major reordering and refurbishment project, undertaken between 2005 and 2010, created a space that doubles as place of worship and village hall. The pews were removed and replaced by wooden chairs and additional stacking chairs. The font was moved into the chancel. Underfloor heating and a new oak floor were installed. A fully accessible toilet and a well-equipped kitchen were put in at the west end, cleverly concealed behind oak doors. A mezzanine level with a glass-fronted rail was inserted; it was used for storage and for ringing the church bell. An audio-visual system and built-in projector screen were added.

The building is now managed – under a 30-year repairing lease from the Diocese – by the Fernham Village Trust, which has responsibility for routine maintenance.

REALISATION

After the village hall was damaged by fire and collapsed in 1955, the villagers used a large barn attached to the pub. When this was converted into a restaurant, they lost their only community space. At the same time regular church services were attracting a small, elderly congregation of about half a dozen and the PCC was increasingly concerned about rising maintenance and heating costs and future usage of the church. The heating system was practically non-existent, and lighting was provided by single bulbs dangling from fabric-covered wires. The roof was beginning to leak and the building was cold and damp. It could not be used for much beyond services, concerts and film nights, as the seventeen 'very hard' pews were all facing forward.

In 2002 the churchwarden, Charles Wickham, circulated a survey stating that the current congregation would be unable to sustain the church as it was. People were asked what they would like to do with the space and whether there would be objections to adapting it to meet modern needs. From the eighty-eight houses, Mr Wickham achieved forty responses, almost all in favour of adapting the building as a combined church and village hall.

At this time the developer of a disused farm on the edge of the village was obliged, as part of the development agreement, to give the Parish Meeting (a smaller version of a Parish Council) a Section 106 disbursement worth £20,000, which could provide seed-corn funding for any project. The villagers agreed that the priority was for a village hall and initially serious consideration was given to putting up a brand new building. There was concern about the expense of maintaining and heating an old building with a high roof. They were aware of what had been done in nearby Little Coxwell: instead of refurbishing their listed church they had commissioned a new, brick-built, eco-friendly building, for which they had obtained SEEDA funding.

However, it was finally recognised that

refurbishing the church to provide a village space would solve two problems at once and that, for a small village, it was better to preserve an old building at its heart rather than commission a new one on the edge of it. The Parish Meeting came on board and granted all the Section 106 money to the project as a measure of village support.

In November 2004 Neil Sutherland, the St John's Treasurer and a chartered civil engineer, was asked to gather together a group of people with the necessary skills in finance and business, fund-raising, and running village events. While some were churchgoers, people were approached for their skills rather than their links to the church. Charles Wickham and the incumbent, the Revd Richard Hancock, were included in an *ex officio* capacity and provided positive and practical support. Project Inspire was set up in due course to run the group as a charitable trust (see below).

Members of the team went to look at five separate church conversions to see how they had been managed and what they had achieved. Oxfordshire Community and Voluntary Action (OCVA) gave advice on project management and on where to apply for funds for the conversion and community benefit works. Other advice came from the South Vale LEADER Programme, the Oxfordshire Rural Community Council and the Trust for Oxfordshire's Environment.

The team's members realised that they needed to highlight the project to their local district and the county, so they briefed the local District Councillor, Yvonne Constance, and the Lord Lieutenant of Oxfordshire. Both were supportive, with Yvonne Constance attending several fund-raising events and the Lord Lieutenant making a formal visit to the project, which helped when applying for local authority grants.

The project ended up with two architects, both local, one who dealt with the roof works and a second commissioned for the conversion works. It was going to be a major reordering, but Neil Sutherland says, 'In fact there were no major dissenters from within the village. There were some who were a bit concerned about removing the pews, but once the context was understood, everybody

Top Exterior from the south-west, September 2005. PHOTO JW

Centre Watching the Royal Wedding, 29 April 2011. PHOTO NEIL SUTHERLAND

Bottom View towards the east end, July 2013. PHOTO BP

kind of fell in behind the project and we marched to the same tune, which was brilliant. We also had very strong support from the Revd Richard Hancock and the churchwarden as well as the support of the Archdeacon of Berkshire, Norman Russell.'

The team understood the need to obtain a faculty for the scheme. However, they found the process lengthy and quite bureaucratic. Extra challenges arose when co-ordinating the seeking of permissions with fund-raising, as many major grant-funding bodies attach tight deadlines to their offers. The team felt that the Victorian Society failed to appreciate that this was basically a 'rescue' project. The Society was trying to reduce the effect of the changes which they felt would have a serious visual impact in such a small church. In their view 'moving the font and the lectern to the chancel would deprive them of their liturgical significance and their role in articulating the space; it would also fill the tiny chancel area with items that are too large for it, resulting in a congested space that would be of limited use for worship'. They insisted on the retention of the low 'rood' walls separating the chancel from the nave. The church felt that they were objecting to almost every facet of the conversion. Negotiations with the Victorian Society held up the project for a year and, at one point, there was a danger that the Big Lottery Fund (BLF) grant of nearly £100,000 would be lost. In the end, the architect went to the society's director responsible for historic churches and negotiated a plan whereby both parties made compromises. The font was moved, but the 'rood' walls were retained, which has prevented the use of the chancel as a stage for plays.

The costs were £220,000 for the roof repairs, which included a complete new set of Cotswold stone tiles, and £184,000 for the conversion, a large amount of money for a small village to find.

In a remarkable feat of solo fund-raising and project management, the churchwarden took charge of sourcing money for the roof repairs. The majority came from English Heritage and other church-supporting charities, among them the Oxfordshire Historic Churches Trust, Garfield Weston Trust, All Churches Trust and Ammco Trust, as well as the Vale of White Horse District Council and the then Regional Development Agency SEEDA.

Project Inspire concentrated on raising the funds for the community part of the project. In November 2007 it won a grant of £94,000 through the Big Lottery Fund and ITV's public voting competition, 'The People's Millions', which brought publicity and increased confidence. Additional funds came from the Trust for Oxfordshire's Environment, the Rural Access to Services Programme, Oxfordshire County Council's Youth Opportunity Fund, Oxfordshire County Council Chill-Out Fund, RWE Npower, the Rotary Club of Faringdon, and Midlands Counties Co-op. Money also came from local benefactors and local fund-raising events such as film nights and talks, which helped to keep people engaged with the project.

After long and careful negotiations with the Diocese, an agreement was reached on the management of the building post-conversion. Project Inspire took on the repairing lease from the Diocese and responsibility for the routine maintenance of the building with an expectation, written into the lease, that if there are major works, Project Inspire will pay 60%, while the church community and PCC will contribute 40%, a ratio of 60:40 reflecting the split between chancel and nave areas.

The converted church, with its brand new roof, was opened in June 2010 by the Earl of Wessex. It has proved to be a versatile venue for everything from dance classes to lectures and meetings, from birthday parties to craft fairs and concerts, and can seat up to 100 people comfortably.

It continues to be a place of worship and the chancel has remained unchanged, although the font was relocated to within the chancel area. As Neil Sutherland says, 'We are getting very used to the building being both a community space and a place of worship. We can have our Burns Night celebrations on a Saturday night and yet by 9am next morning everything is "facing front" ready for morning worship.'

At a meeting of villagers in May 2012, it was agreed that Project Inspire and another group, the Fernham Events Committee, should join forces to become the Fernham Village Trust. The charitable trust, set up as a company limited by guarantee to limit the liability of the Trustees and to meet funding criteria, runs village events and now manages the use of St John's and Fernham Village Hall by the community and the church and covers the running costs. The management committee is elected every year at the Trust's AGM and members serve for a year.

The PCC pays to hire the building for its services and other church activities, such as weddings and funerals. It also raises funds for its annual parish share, which goes towards clergy costs, and helps to cover the mission and outreach of the church.

Neil Sutherland explains that 'we are now four years into our 30-year lease agreement with the Diocese and it is working well. The Trust and the church work well together and set up many joint events such as the village fête, where the church organises the refreshments, which raises funds for them. Other events such as the fireworks are put on solely by the Trust and help to generate funds, some of which pay for the building insurance.'

The aim is to keep the hall hire as cheap as is cost-effective. Currently it can be hired for £15 per hour (including car park use), with a reduced rate of £7.50 per hour for Fernham villagers. A heating surcharge of £1.50 an hour is added between November and March.

Funds brought to the Trust by the Events Committee and Project Inspire, plus some grants, have enabled the completion of a car park. This is adjacent to the south-east corner of the churchyard, on glebe land given by the Diocese. It has improved disabled access across the churchyard to the south entrance and has made the hall more marketable to outside groups. The building can also be hired for private events. Space has been created in the churchyard for a large marquee, available for hire from the Trust along with tables and chairs, in which wedding breakfasts or buffet meals can be provided.

Neil Sutherland says the project has brought the community together. 'It is still a delightful little village church and when there is a service, the only visible change is that the font has moved and that there are now slightly more comfortable chairs than the previous pews. Now, it has been given a new lease of life. Prior to the conversion it was half a story as it was just a church with the ability to run one or two minor village events; now it has developed to become a focus of the community.'

The facilities at the west end, July 2013. The door on the left of the kitchen leads to the staircase to the upper floor. PHOTO BP

CHALLENGES

The biggest challenges for the project team were dealing with the requirements of obtaining a faculty and negotiating a 30-year lease from the Diocese of Oxford, as well as reaching a workable agreement with the Victorian Society on the reordering of the building.

LESSONS LEARNED

A major frustration has been the failure of the new heating system to work efficiently. It seems it was not correctly designed to suit a wooden floor and it has been expensive to maintain a sufficient temperature in the winter. It has been registered as a building defect and the Trust is waiting for an alternative scheme to be proposed. With hindsight, the Project Team would have insisted that the architect employed a specialist heating engineer or consultant.

BEST PIECE OF ADVICE

A project of this complexity will need a range of specific skills. Those skills which are not present in the congregation can often be found in the wider community.

WEBSITE

The village and church share the same website http://www.fernham.info/

St Thomas of Canterbury, Goring-on-Thames

I think before it was probably viewed as a place for a select few, and being dark and dingy, it was not a place people would rush to. Now it's light and bright and used for lots of activities; but for the scheme, other 'non-religious' events could not have been accommodated, however well-intentioned my predecessors were. The Revd Mark Blamey

Goring is a large village with a population of around 3,500 on the Thames in South Oxfordshire.

The Grade 1 listed church has retained overall its eleventh-century Romanesque style. It was originally dedicated to the Virgin Mary, as was the nuns' priory, founded in the early years of the twelfth century, which surrounded the church on three sides. The nuns built their own church as an extension of the parish church, which involved demolishing the parish church apse. At the Dissolution of the Monasteries in the 1530s, most of the priory's buildings including its church were razed. The wall dividing the churches became the east wall of the parish church. The foundations of the priory church and other buildings were excavated in 1887 and the present apse was built on the original foundation in 1888 to the designs of Ben Corser.

THE PROJECT

Initial thinking for this project, which was originally designed to mark the new millennium, began in the early 1990s. The major reordering and building of the extension took place between October 2008 and September 2009. An underfloor heating system was installed, with a new breathable stone floor laid on a 'Limecrete' foundation. Within the chancel the choir stalls were removed and the rood screen relocated, which has created a recital space and a new communion table on a new stone dais. Throughout, the pews and stalls were replaced with purpose-made stackable chairs and pews.

The Canterbury Room forms an extension attached to the south side of the church over a portion of the north cloister of the ancient priory. This houses toilets, a kitchen and a large room that can be subdivided by a folding wooden screen. It is connected to the main body of the church via the reopened and raised Nuns' Doorway.

REALISATION

The church had undergone two major restorations during the nineteenth century. In the winter of 1848–49, a new young incumbent, the Revd (later Dr) John Fell, influenced by the reforming Oxford Movement, removed the west gallery and replaced the Georgian box pews with rather poor-quality ones, described by his successor as 'deal seats'. Mr Fell's aim was to increase capacity and at the same time get rid of the rentable pews and extend the free provision for the poor. In 1888 the Revd Henry Littlewood and the architect Ben Corser, advised by the diocesan architect J. Scott, constructed the new east end apse, installing a new organ chamber and organ in the north aisle.

In the 1990s the church was acknowledged to be dark, gloomy and damp. The PCC wanted to create a warmer and more welcoming space, literally, as the Victorian heating system was inefficient and used large pipes that people had to step over to get into the pews. The floor had different levels and consisted of different materials. The goal, which involved improving accessibility throughout and providing new facilities and flexible spaces for multiple uses, was to reinforce connections and better serve the wider community.

In 2000 the organ was refurbished and a new sound and lighting system installed, but further work

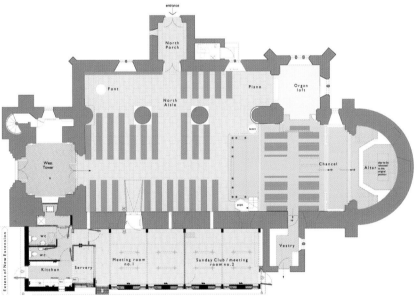

Top Exterior from the south after the extension, September 2009.
PHOTO DAVID STEWART, ACANTHUS CLEWS ARCHITECTS

Centre Plan showing the layout after reordering, September 2009.
PHOTO ACANTHUS CLEWS ARCHITECTS

Right The interior at floor level before works done, looking towards the east end, showing pews and heating pipes, 2008.
PHOTO BOB GREGORY

took longer. Initial proposals for further changes were limited by local opposition and restrictions from the planning authorities. Only half the pews could be removed and only a narrow extension built rather than a broad room. The main entrance was to move to the west tower and access to the extension was to have been through a south door from the tower room, where there was an existing toilet and cramped kitchen built in the 1970s. The tower room is 20ft high, with a lofty vaulted ceiling, but it proved difficult to create an accessible area because the tenth-century floor of the tower is two deep steps below the Victorian floor level of the nave, which was built over graves from different centuries.

It was also clear that the proposed extension would not really be big enough for additional activities. The project was losing momentum, not helped by an interregnum; nowhere near enough money had been raised.

In 2004 a new vicar, the Revd Mark Blamey, a former surveyor, arrived and brought in architects Acanthus Clews to reconsider the scheme. They undertook a feasibility study and drew up several different options, which were presented at public meetings to the whole parish. The aim was, says Mr Blamey, to show the congregation and the community 'how seriously the church takes its mission because it was proposing a modern building which would respect and enhance the church as a place of beauty and sanctuary which is loved'.

A degree of unhappiness was expressed at these public meetings. Some voiced concern that the project would set up competition with the village hall. More difficult was the fierce opposition to the proposed loss of the 1848–49 pews (even though they were of poor quality), and dismay at disturbing graves during the installation of the new floor and the building of the extension. Some felt so strongly that they took their objections almost up to a Consistory Court before withdrawing. Others, now that they have seen the finished product, are much more appreciative. A few remain unconvinced and now worship at the more traditional St Mary's, Streatley.

However, there was a growing general acceptance. The 2005 Goring Parish Plan recorded a recommendation that action should be taken within

the next five years 'to make wider use of the Parish Church'. Mr Blamey acknowledges that this is in part thanks to the hard work put in by the previous vicar in consulting the village about the earlier proposals. The new project was taken forward under the title of 'St Thomas's Builds for Tomorrow'.

The agreed plan was to re-open the Nuns' Doorway in the south aisle, which had originally led directly into the priory cloister. The height of the arch was extended in 2009, as the floor of the church must have been at least two feet below the present level, and the doorway was made accessible by a ramp and rails. The extension itself was to be built over the footprint of the historic priory cloister, on a raised raft to protect sixteen graves, which the planners were very careful to survey and care for.

The new building has a lightweight glulam timber post-and-beam frame supporting the oak and lime-render wall panels and the standing seam zinc roof. The design incorporates sustainable construction methods and building materials throughout, and a passive solar-driven ventilation system. The exterior is natural English oak and stone. Timber shutters had to be installed, as Goring has suffered from occasional Friday night vandalism. The Victorian pebbledash on the external south wall was removed.

Inside, a new floor was installed with underfloor heating. The damp problem was solved by removing the Victorian rendering in the nave and replacing it with lime render painted white. Originally, the church wanted to re-site the 1910 rood screen at the west end with the aim of restoring the classic Romanesque view from there down to the east apse. The DAC, although supporting the rest of the scheme, insisted the rood screen be kept where it was as being of special significance, since it was designed and erected by Perry Stone (who also designed the Parish Room, now the village hall) and was carved on the Isle of Wight from oak reputedly salvaged from one of the ships of the line at Trafalgar, HMS *Thunderer*. However, they did allow it to be moved by about 20ft further eastwards, which has created a small high chancel area within the 1888 apse.

The removal of the choir stalls and the communion rail has cleared the space for a new communion table and recital space on a new stone

Above Interior showing the new furniture, March 2012.
PHOTO BERNARD NOVELL

Right Detail of the ramp leading up to the Nuns' Doorway and into the Canterbury Room, September 2009.
PHOTO DAVID STEWART, ACANTHUS CLEWS ARCHITECTS

Below Interior of the Canterbury Room looking through the kitchen hatch, September 2009.
PHOTO DAVID STEWART, ACANTHUS CLEWS ARCHITECTS

dais extending into the nave. The high altar is now used only on special occasions and for weddings. A member of the church said that one of the surprising by-products of the reordering has been that 'as a church, we are now much more informal and relaxed'.

This has been a gradual process: a nave altar had previously been experimented with. However, holding services in the primary school while the works were ongoing enabled the congregation to look again at how they worshipped, and, incidentally, also helped build stronger relationships between the church and school.

The font was moved from the tower, which had been the baptistery, and placed in the nave in front of the north aisle, thereby bringing baptisms back into the main body of the church.

Interestingly, the PCC also took the decision – after an open meeting, with furniture samples, and a decisive paper vote – to replace the poor-quality 1850s pews with pew-like benches. They were made by furniture specialist Bates and Lambourne of Milton, a local Oxfordshire firm, of good-quality English oak. Designed in consultation with the church, the pews come in differing lengths from one to four seats, but all are stackable and all interlinkable. They were obviously expensive, but the churchwarden, borrowing an idea he came across in his daughter's church, offered the chance to anyone in the village to dedicate a new pew in memory of people or events for £250 per seat. This raised the required funds, and the church continues to receive requests for a dedication and to buy a pew.

The immediate feeling on entering is one of light produced by the new lighting, pale oak furniture, white walls and pale new floor. The extension is of modern design, but the traditional materials and good craftsmanship match in quality the Grade 1 listed building. The Sunday School now uses the extension. There is a drop-down screen at the east end linked to a camera so it can be used for overflow at important services and large weddings and funerals as well as large community meetings. The church and the Canterbury Room are used in many different ways: for concerts, Pilates classes, art exhibitions, films and children's parties. Different kinds of people are now coming into the building, among them those

who feel able to just come in and sit quietly now that they have attended an event. Goring has several community facilities including the village hall, the Community Centre, the Social Club and the Free Church. Mark Blamey stresses that the village has done its research and shown that it can sustain all these community facilities. When public money has been sought for the church and the village hall, which was also refurbished recently, both projects have been able to make the case that there are about 100 to 150 voluntary groups who all need venues.

Mr Blamey is very clear that, rather than being set apart, the church is a civic building belonging to all members of the community. Moreover, the grants awarded for the project meant that 'I've had to sign documents that compel my successors in perpetuity to make available the Canterbury Room for everyone within reasonable hours. That's good and although some in the faith community say they would prefer it if the church could raise the money for itself and totally regulate use of the building, I prefer the former, because that's our mission. And at times, over the last couple of years, it has been quite tricky re-engaging with a new building for all intents and purposes and, moreover, a new or renewed relationship with the community. All of a sudden it was usable, all of a sudden people wanted to come into it and use it for non-religious purposes and that is great. It does lead to some complexity and negotiation, but that's what we are meant to be doing.'

He added, 'While in faith and with hope a great deal can be accomplished, as a jaded surveyor I wonder how strongly you can play the reordering project as mission line, because the potential is there, certainly, but in and of itself you are talking about bricks and mortar.' In September 2013, the church put on a month of outreach events entitled 'Your guide to Operation Sat-Nav', which invited people to explore faith and spirituality.

CHALLENGES
The total cost of the refurbishment was £350,000, plus £500,000 for the extension. The furniture came to a further £56,000. The project benefited initially from employing a fund-raiser who helped develop a funding strategy, and then the current

Right Children in church.
PHOTO GORING CHURCH

Below Pews stacked.
PHOTO BATES AND LAMBOURNE

curate took over. Two big grants were awarded by SODC (£133,000) and WREN (£50,000). About £450,000 came from the congregation and the village via donations, bequests and fund-raising events. The Revd Mark Blamey says, 'There was some very selfless giving from the congregation and the wider village responded very generously. It was humbling for me to get envelopes coming through the door after we had visited every house with people who ostensibly had no close connection but for whom the building was important.'

LESSONS LEARNED
Beware of spiralling building costs. Because of the increase in scope of the works and rising costs in the construction industry, costs increased substantially.

Make good use of local newsletters. The PCC was given a monthly space in the free local newspaper, *The Goring Gap News*, in which they explained the proposals and gave updates on progress.

BEST PIECE OF ADVICE
Expect and accept that you will face some opposition. This is inevitable, especially if it is a major reordering, even though you are trying to restore the building's usefulness and survival. This can be very painful and you can lose people. You need to be resolute, while continually trying to articulate your vision, consult and listen to feedback. And, over time, one of the joys is seeing people with the courage to say 'I was opposed to this, now I see why you've done it.'

(Research into the history of previous restorations at St Thomas's by local historian Dr Garry Alder has put this into perspective: objections to proposals in the 1880s were led by local influential parishioner General James Fife and the previous incumbent Dr Fell, and at one point the current incumbent was accused of suppressing criticism and advice from the diocesan architect.)

ST PETER, HOOK NORTON

This is a place of worship and community and fellowship and we have tried to keep it that way. If we are not careful all thoughts of it being a sacred place about God can easily be lost by people who just come in and use it as another venue. The Revd John Acreman

Hook Norton is a village of between 2,500 and 3,000 inhabitants about six miles north of Chipping Norton in north-west Oxfordshire, on the edge of the Cotswolds. St Peter's is in the High Street, on a rise, in the centre of the village opposite the Sun Inn.

The Grade 1 listed church is Saxon in origin, but predominantly Norman, which is apparent in the Romanesque chancel and north transept. A spacious nave was added in the late fourteenth century and the pinnacled perpendicular west tower in the sixteenth century. St Peter's also houses the village's original fire engine, known as 'The Sentinel', which was last used in 1896.

THE PROJECT

In 1998, at a cost of £137,000, the church tower was glazed in and two toilets and a kitchen were installed on the ground floor, with a meeting room on the first floor and the ringing chamber above.

Access was improved with the installation of a lift to allow disabled people to enter the facilities, and the new sound system included a hearing loop.

During the second phase, the pews were removed and replaced with chairs. The Font Café was created with chairs and tables at the west end of the south aisle, near the facilities.

Since then the Raise the Roof Committee has raised in the region of £250,000 to replace the chancel and the south aisle roofs. The current phase, led by the Plaster and Paint St Peter's Committee, is busy raising £150,000 to restore and repair the interior ceilings and walls.

REALISATION

The reordering and restoration of St Peter's has gone through several phases over the last twenty years. The PCC reached agreement with the DAC in the early 1990s to remove the rood screen, which had come from a bombed-out church in Kidderminster in 1947, and the very cramped choir stalls from the transept area between the chancel and the nave.

This allowed a raised dais to be created in the empty space, which has provided scope for all sorts of activities including concerts, theatrical performances and school presentations. These changes encouraged the PCC to start thinking about how else it could open up the building for more flexible use, which in the long term would provide it with a more sustainable future.

It was agreed that installing toilets and a kitchen was key. Discussions with the DAC started in 1998 and originally the proposal was to put the facilities in the north aisle. There was initial reluctance to move the early-nineteenth-century church clock at the base of the tower. The solution was to put the clock in the village museum, where it is now a much appreciated working exhibit.

This meant that toilets and kitchen could be situated at the foot of the west tower, with an upper room above, retaining the ringing chamber above that. Fortunately the bells were arranged with a long enough drop for a mezzanine floor to be inserted to create the upper room without affecting the bell-ringers. The upper room is now used by the Sunday School and family groups.

An early decision was made to glaze in the archway into the tower so that the west window could still be seen and people in the upper room could see down into the church. It looks very elegant and works well. Because the facilities are in the tower room, there is plenty of space at the west end to set up chairs and tables for the Font Café, which is open to all on Tuesday and Saturday mornings, manned by volunteers and frequented principally by people from the village.

There were problems of access, as there are three steps up to the floor of the tower. The PCC looked at the possibility of lowering the floor, but this was deemed impractical. It was decided instead to install a lift to take a wheelchair up and down the steps. The Revd John Acreman explains that not only is it unobtrusive, but it has proved a great advantage to those who find steps awkward: 'People if they so wish can now come in through the west door and not have to negotiate steps at the south entrance.'

It was decided to provide more suitable seating arrangements. Late Victorian pews had been replaced in 1911 by pine clerical benches, stained dark brown and by now full of woodworm. These were removed in 2006. The PCC, with very helpful advice from the DAC, decided upon wooden chairs and specified that the cushioned seating and backs should be rich burgundy, the colour of St Peter. The 108 wooden chairs cost £7,560 plus VAT. Additional stacking chairs were purchased to cater for larger events. Some of the better-preserved pews have been moved and placed around the sides of the Font Café area at the west end.

The Victorian Society raised no objection to the removal of the pews, and there was an unlooked-for benefit in that it showed to great advantage the Victorian memorial window in the south aisle. The Society was also pleased that the PCC agreed to leave the late Victorian granulite floor in place around the Font Café area and elsewhere in the church.

The PCC ensured that everyone was kept informed of every stage of the process through the village newsletter and as part of fund-raising events. There was very little opposition from the village, and while there were those who did not want the pews taken out, many now agree that the chairs are much easier to move and more comfortable. Seven years on, despite constant use, the chairs show no sign

Top Exterior from the south, July 2013. PHOTO JW

Centre Interior showing the pews but after the removal of the rood screen and choir stalls, March 2007. PHOTO JW

Bottom Wider view of the interior, showing new chairs and others stacked behind a screen in the north aisle, July 2013. PHOTO BP

of wear and tear. Notwithstanding this success, the visitors' book was removed for a time because of adverse comments written after the chairs had been installed. It was felt that they were made by visitors from elsewhere and were not a true reflection of how people in the locality, whose church it is, felt about the changes.

In 2011/2012, the Raise the Roof Committee raised around £250,000 to replace the chancel and south aisle roofs. The current phase, led by the Plaster and Paint St Peter's Committee, is raising £150,000 to restore and repair the interior ceilings and walls. At the same time, after fifteen years of heavy use, the tower facilities need to be redecorated. 'This', says Mr Acreman, 'is a good thing, because it's worn out rather than rusted out.' In the autumn of 2013, the floor below the organ collapsed and so yet more funds have to be raised.

This illustrates a common situation. John Acreman has been Rector at St Peter's for twenty-one years and 'doesn't know a time when I haven't been raising funds for the upkeep of the church. It's a credit to a village of this size that they have been constantly stepping up to the plate for the last twenty-odd years.' However, he acknowledges that it is becoming more difficult because the current generation doesn't have the same connection to the church as previous generations.

The reorderings have been a success and the church is now being used by the community throughout the year. Thanks to the chairs, the space can be adapted for a wide variety of different occasions, whether the village Flower Show, the annual November Craft Fair, a concert, a dinner dance or the Midsummer Ball. For a big wedding or funeral all the chairs can be used, while for a small event fewer chairs are put out so that people don't feel 'they are rattling about'. The church has a good relationship with the Sun Inn opposite, which provides catering in the building for some events, while for others people move over to the pub for refreshments. Every now and then the PCC delivers flyers to every house in the village to ensure that everyone knows about specific events such as St Peter's Day.

Mr Acreman believes wider usage has changed for the better the way the village views the church. 'I think that some of the younger people, those with young families, who have come to a dance with a bar in the church – and they are the age group when you didn't do that sort of thing and now you do – have been quite taken by the fact that the church is making the effort, and it is refreshing to them.'

Along with many other church leaders, he is less certain about whether this wider community use is going to bring in sufficient income to sustain the building in the long term. He says that the church doesn't want to be seen as a money-making organisation so does not charge commercial rates, but that the running and maintenance costs of the building have increased. 'Nowadays, people expect to be comfortable and the heating and lighting to be on and for there to be continuous hot water. We have to pay for cleaners now that the church is being used for a wider and messier variety of activities.' That said, many more people are using and enjoying the building, and he says 'their presence in the church means far more than their money'.

For the worshipping community, this raises the concern that in order to sustain them we are in danger of turning our churches into tourist attractions and commercial venues rather than places of worship where God's people meet and where the gospel is preached, and they are possibly losing their specific role within the local community. Getting the balance right is important. If there is music, for instance, the rector will always make sure that it is appropriate, which to date it always has been. It is greatly appreciated that those who use the building have always been respectful and always help to clear up. There have been unexpected benefits. For one of the dinner dances, a local man organised a light show which Mr Acreman says 'gave a tasteful nightclub feel to the church, but it was so stunning, he was invited to produce a light show for the Christmas Eve carol service, which was equally impressive and beautifully done, and very well received'.

CHALLENGES

The main challenge is money: first raising sufficient and secondly, because of the complexity of finance and accounting, needing people with financial experience who can keep control of the budget.

LESSONS LEARNED

Work out how long you imagine the work will take to complete, and then double it!

Do not expect the incumbent to manage the project. Involve lots of people by setting up an overall committee, supported by subcommittees responsible for different areas. The work will then be shared and owned by those taking responsibility for making it happen. Ensure that there is good communication between all committees.

BEST PIECE OF ADVICE

It is important to get the right contractor, and obtaining recommendations from the DAC is a good way of identifying reliable and experienced firms.

WEBSITE

http://www.stpeters-hooknorton.org.uk/

The Font Café area at the west end of the south aisle, adjacent to the glazed-in tower housing the facilities, July 2013. PHOTO JW

Below left Appeal notice outside the church, July 2013. PHOTO BP

Below The glazed-in west tower and lift, July 2013. PHOTO BP

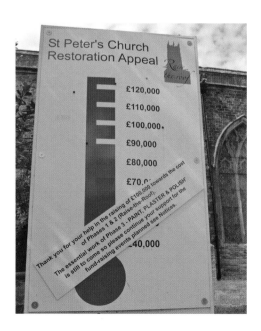

St Mary the Virgin, Kirtlington

We did a lot of measuring up to see what could be done in various places. We moved the organ mentally to every corner of the church. The discussions went on for a long time with everybody having different views, but it ensured we were finally able to settle on a scheme that met all our requirements. Margaret Forey, former churchwarden

Kirtlington is a village about nine miles north of Oxford with 450 households and a population of 1,000. It is the largest village in the seven-parish Akeman benefice, with the largest church. Right in the centre of the village, the church is hidden from the main road.

Only the imposts of the chancel arch survive of the Saxon building. The present Grade II* listed church consists of a nave with north and south aisles, a central tower between the nave and chancel and a south chapel. The east and west tower arches are early twelfth-century, while the nave and its aisles are mid-thirteenth-century. The original tower was demolished in the late eighteenth century and rebuilt in neo-Norman style by Benjamin Ferrey in 1853. At the same time, the box pews and gallery were removed. The chancel was restored by Sir George Gilbert Scott in 1877.

THE PROJECT

A complete internal refurbishment was required to introduce modern facilities into the church. During 2008 and 2009, an accessible toilet with scope for baby-changing and a flower-arranging area with sink and storage were installed in the north-west corner, enclosed within oak-framed, 8ft-high glass partitions. York stone flooring with underfloor heating was laid throughout the nave and aisles and radiators put in the chancel and chapel. Two types of new chairs were introduced and a new storage facility, including a rail for choir robes, was fitted beneath the tower. More recently, a new lighting scheme was put in and new choir stalls provided.

REALISATION

In 1994 the PCC received a legacy of £60,000, with the suggestion that it might be spent on a toilet. The PCC liked the idea, but once discussions began an influential local resident urged the building of a large two-storey extension with an ambitious range of facilities, promising to find funding if the PCC contributed £30,000. Arguments raged for some years and when eventually, by the narrowest of margins, the PCC agreed, two members resigned and a petition against the extension was immediately started; within a week it had almost 200 signatures. The archdeacon vetoed the scheme as divisive, so the £8,000 already spent on plans was wasted. In 2004, a new subcommittee was formed to think again, concentrating on the existing building.

By this time, the old boiler was not working properly and, as Margaret Forey, churchwarden at the time, describes it: 'If we'd been a factory, we wouldn't have been allowed to operate in those conditions. The flower arrangers used to work for an hour or so and then, seriously frozen, would have to go home and get hot drinks and huddle by fires just to warm up.'

The dark nineteenth-century pews were agreed to be of poor quality, uncomfortable and riddled with woodworm. The red and black floor tiles were cracked, and worms had been seen emerging between them. The church was not connected to the mains and water for coffee had to be brought in.

One key practical issue was that, after the services, coffee had to be served in the north aisle because the font with its large base blocked access to unused space near the main south entrance. This meant

Above right Exterior from the west, 2004.
PHOTO JW

Above left Looking across the nave to the north-west corner before works done, August 2005.
PHOTO ACANTHUS CLEWS ARCHITECTS

Right Close-up of the facilities showing oak frame and glass infill panels, July 2013. PHOTO BP

Below Interior looking across the nave towards the facilities at the north-west corner, July 2009, showing the two types of chairs in use.
PHOTO DAVID STEWART, ACANTHUS CLEWS ARCHITECTS

that after services regulars would know to go to the north aisle, while newcomers or the shy would often disappear out of the south door before anyone had the chance to welcome them.

The PCC wanted to make the church more comfortable, accessible and welcoming to all. The greater part of the congregation was in its seventies and eighties, and the future of the church was in doubt. It was felt that opening up the building for wider use by the community would provide an important link with the non-churchgoing population, and help the church and village to become more closely integrated.

Feeling it important to keep the wider community fully informed, Margaret Forey, who had opposed the earlier scheme, wrote a piece for the *Village News* with the aim of providing as impartial an account as possible of what had happened, but reiterating why the PCC felt it was necessary to make changes. Learning from what happened when the wider community was not consulted and how rumours can take off, she continued throughout the project to write regular articles. There were still those who opposed the removal of the pews and the idea of a toilet. However, the PCC felt it had to keep moving forward and spent many months rethinking what it was trying to achieve and how best to introduce modern facilities. It continued working with the architects Acanthus Clews, who had been originally brought in to design the extension. Eventually it was agreed that there was sufficient space within the existing building to accommodate all the requirements, and the DAC approved the new plans.

The entire project, apart from a final redecoration, for which a further £10,000–£11,000 is being raised, has cost £305,088.

Thanks to an excellent local fund-raising committee, £154,838 was raised directly from the community either in gifts or through events. Grants were also applied for, but only £25,250 came by this means. Margaret Forey says that many funders seemed to feel that because Kirtlington has a village hall, even though it is often fully booked, they were not prepared to support a second community building. However, two more legacies came in, bringing the total from this source to £125,000. From

the start it was intended that the work should be done in stages as funds allowed, partly so that donors should be encouraged by seeing results, partly to prevent costs rising faster than the fund-raising could match.

Phase 1 in 2008 was the installation of the toilet and flower-arrangers' area in the north-west corner, replacing the choir vestry. Plans for mains drainage were found to be too costly, so instead of a cesspit, for which regular usage is preferable and which incurs running costs, a trench arch drainage system was installed. This was cheaper, in spite of the extra £5,000 needed to call in an osteo-archaeologist when digging unexpectedly disturbed thirty-six complete skeletons. The system works by creating a void between two shallow blockwork walls, forming a long sand-filled trench that slopes gently away from the connected sewage outlet; it is covered with paving slabs and then with earth. Material flowing into it is naturally degraded by worms and other biological activity.

The new facilities were enclosed within a purpose-built box made up of a simple light oak frame and 8ft-high, 12mm-thick glass infill panels. The panels retain the light turquoise hue of natural untreated glass, emphasised by the white ceramic backing. The walls were painted and the font, minus its ugly, inconvenient base, was moved to a position in the north aisle below the fifteenth-century wall painting. A children's area was created nearby. The choir robes, the big Victorian safe, the cleaning materials and other items from the choir vestry were rehoused in a new storage area under the tower, with mesh doors that allow the passage of air.

In 2009, in Phase 2, the pews were removed. They were first offered to the village and specialist salvage companies; only a few were sold, but the rest were donated to a charity that had a use for the wood.

The Victorian plain red tile and dark oak flooring in the nave and aisles was replaced by a York stone floor. Underfloor heating was laid throughout the nave and beneath the tower, with top-up radiators by the doors and in the children's area, and radiators installed in the chancel and chapel.

Two kinds of chairs were purchased, part-funded by being individually sponsored by local people. As

Above The east window reflected in the glass covering the decorated Victorian cast-iron heating grille; new storage cupboards also visible, November 2011. PHOTO LIBBY RUSSELL

Centre A Pilates class taking place; the glass box in the north-west corner also shown, 2012. PHOTO TERRI HOPKINS

Below Setting up the 2012 Art Exhibition.
PHOTO SYLVIA OLDCORN

primary seating for the front half of the nave, there are now sixty-four cushioned 'American white ash' seats by Irish Contract Seating, with an integral book rack, and a flower motif, copied from the altar rail by George Gilbert Scott, carved into the backrest of each chair. They are upholstered in a turquoise fabric to complement the pale turquoise hue of the glass, and the same colour in a deeper shade is found on the organ pipes in the opposite corner. The chairs, stackable in threes, clip together at the front, and can be arranged in curves or straight lines as needed. In fact, the chairs are heavy and do not slip on the stone floor, and the clips have proved unnecessary.

As secondary seating, the PCC purchased eighty

lighter metal-framed stacking chairs with the seats and backs also in white ash, and the same motifs carved on the backs. They are normally kept stacked high on three trolleys at the west end, thus allowing a large space for socialising after services, but they can easily be set out for weddings, funerals, and other special occasions. They can be set up or stacked by two people in around twenty minutes. The total seating capacity is thus about 140 people, about the same as provided by the pews.

Careful thought was given throughout to the choice of colours. As well as the complementary turquoise of the glass, organ pipes and upholstered chairs, the pale ash wood of the chairs and the pale floor tone with the stonework and white walls. The effect is to create a wonderful unified interior of light and calm with a sense of spaciousness. Margaret Forey says, 'Before it was very dark and there was a sort of dark tunnel leading up to the chancel. Now you can really see it is a beautiful church and you notice the pillars and the arches in a way that you never did before.'

Beneath the tower, the nineteenth-century decorative cast-iron heating grille has been retained and covered with three-ply laminated glass which is flush with the surrounding stone flooring. An unexpected benefit is that from the nave the whole length of the large Victorian east window can be seen reflected in the glass. The effect is visually stunning; it lightens up the whole tower area, and draws the eye up to the chancel and altar, which otherwise might seem rather cut off from the body of the church.

After a gap to enable more fund-raising, in 2012 a new lighting system was installed in Phase 3 and choir pews in 2013 as Phase 4. Plans for a servery in cupboards in the south-west corner have been shelved for financial reasons, and because the present arrangements are adequate.

This is a church in which, for most regular services, the high altar continues to be used in the chancel, which remains unchanged. The new seating has added significant flexibility for other occasions such as, Margaret Forey says, 'when we have a memorial service down in the nave; we put the chairs in a semicircle around the nave altar and people light candles for those who have died'.

The congregation now appreciates the comfortable seating, the new facilities and the building always being warm. Coffee is now served in the space newly accessible in the south-west corner, making it easy and natural for visitors to pause and stay instead of leaving. The organists have reported that the acoustics have improved greatly since the removal of the pews.

There is a monthly coffee morning, and other events have included concerts, a dramatic performance, and a conference; the church has been used by children's music and dance groups and an exercise class. Gradually other groups are coming forward, seeing the potential in using the space because of its special ambience. At the suggestion of a villager, there is an art exhibition every other year and exhibits are put up all over the church as far as the altar rails.

Sadly, the most recent quinquennial inspection has revealed the necessity for roof repairs, so once the redecoration is completed fund-raising will have to begin again.

LESSONS LEARNED
Think through at the beginning everything you want to do and plan with that in mind, otherwise you may have limited your options later on.

BEST PIECE OF ADVICE
Local musicians were asked to give advice on the provision and location of sufficient power points. Double sockets were installed by all four pillars at the same time as the underfloor heating.

WEBSITE
http://www.akemanbenefice.org.uk/st-mary-the-virgin-kirtlington/

New Road Baptist Church, Oxford

We aim to provide a peaceful and friendly environment in which you can rest and relax over a cup of tea or coffee. There is also space in the chapel for you to pray or meditate or you can take a walk around the chapel with a prayer guide. On some days short worship services take place to which you are welcome if you want to join in.

Notice on front door of church

New Road Baptist Church is situated on Bonn Square, right at the edge of the main shopping area in Oxford, with several bus stops nearby.

There has been a chapel on the site from 1721, but the core of the existing two-storey Grade II listed building was erected in 1798. Major enlargements and improvements took place in 1819, when the pillars and architrave on the front were added.

THE PROJECT

In 1982 a major internal reordering took place. The organ was moved, the pews were taken out and the baptistery was built. At about the same time, four floors of new halls and rooms were built on the premises, and additional adjacent premises were secured on long-term lease from the Council. In 2008 the forecourt of the church was opened to form part of the new Bonn Square redevelopment project, which placed the church at the heart of one of Oxford's public squares.

Various repairs have been undertaken over the last few years, including emergency repairs to the roof and ceiling and subsequent redecoration in 2012 and 2013. The opportunity was taken to put in new lighting.

The responsibility for running a Baptist church lies with the church membership, with decisions taken at members' meetings. The church deacons are legally the Trustees.

REALISATION

The mission statement of this congregation is a commitment to praying and working for the peace and well-being of the city of Oxford through worship, witness and service. Over the last thirty years, the church has been finding creative ways of reaching out to the people who live in, work in and visit Oxford. Since the early 1980s there have been four rooms of varying size for hire, including a café area, adjacent to the church but with a separate entrance. The sanctuary itself can seat 350 and is regularly used for concerts and lectures.

Hiring out the building is important, says the Minister, the Revd Kat Bracewell, 'as being able to offer space for groups and activities is a real way of providing a service to the community and it brings in income for sustaining the building'. The members are currently looking at usage of all the rooms to see how they can realise their full potential, and developing plans for refurbishment.

While they have always had regular users such as Alcoholics Anonymous and Narcotics Anonymous, they have more recently been looking at how they can turn the 'Peace to the City' part of their mission statement into more of a reality and are seeking partnerships with Oxford organisations holding similar aims of peace and justice. They are aware that their central location is a key benefit they offer and it allows them to be flexible about the organisations they choose to support. Kat Bracewell says, 'If someone is trying to do a project and is having problems securing funding and cannot meet all costs, then, if we see the benefit of it, and can be part of it and it fits in with "Peace in the City", we will provide that space. It is very liberating to be able to cut loose from some of the official structures that we normally have to live in.'

The members do not accept bookings from organisations, among them some multinational corporations, that they believe are involved in unethical businesses. They have made the statutory agencies aware of the facilities, which have proved of interest to organisations based outside Oxford that need a temporary central base for a specific project.

In 2013, the Children's Society moved their Oxford office into the top floor. Kat Bracewell says, 'We are just really excited about the opportunity to support their work with vulnerable families, often refugee families.' Some of the new activities bring in no direct income. For example, Ms Bracewell says, 'We have just developed a partnership with the Youth Offending Team of Oxfordshire County Council who run restorative justice activities at the church. This is a service we provide for free just because we want to be part of restorative justice work.'

In 2008 the church gave permission for a peace plaque to be put up outside on the side wall, which has become a meeting place for people of 'all faiths and none' to hold peace vigils on significant days and when people want to gather at times of world crisis.

For many years the church had been talking with the City Council about the use of Bonn Square, the large square of which it owns the lower part directly in front. Both the church and that part of the square were largely hidden behind a fence and trees. The council owned the higher part to the left of the church and was keen to find ways of improving its presentation and use. In 2007 an agreement was signed by the church and the City Council. While each party retains ownership of its half, a joint Management Committee has been set up to look after and develop the whole square.

The fence and trees were removed and the newly paved Bonn Square was opened on 28 November 2008. As Kat Bracewell explains, 'It was the beginning of a whole new era where the church is highly visible and right out there in the heart of the community and used in a very different way. We now feel very much part of this square and people are coming right up to the door of the church and we try to be out there wherever we can.'

The Management Committee, two members of the church and two from the City Council, came up with criteria for events that take place in the square. The overall objective is to ensure Bonn Square is used and enjoyed by the community. The policy has been to steer away from street trading, which could have provided an easy income, and to create a place for local cultural events, entertainment and space for local charities to undertake community engagement.

The church organises events several times a year using its part of the square to encourage community involvement, and these are, explains Ms Bracewell, 'sort of light mission activity which people can engage with'.

In 2010 five events were put on over five weeks based on the Baptist Union Five Core Values – Prophetic, Inclusive, Sacrificial, Missionary, Worshipping – in which an interactive activity was created for each core value that explained its meaning in today's society.

For one week, a large lorry called 'Escape to Safety' stood in front of the church offering an interactive experience of what it means to be an asylum-seeker and representing what it is to be part of a Prophetic Community.

On Valentine's Day, the church members set up a 'graffiti' wall and encouraged people to add their own endings to the phrase 'Love is...' as a way of starting conversations on what it means to create an Inclusive Community.

To represent Sacrificial Community, they set up a Faith on Water activity where, using a bicycle on a stand and a hand pump, people were reminded of the importance of water by being asked to pretend they were cycling for water, pumping a pailful, and then cycling back with it. Recording people's times created an involvement from young men who kept coming back to try to beat their own time.

For Kat Bracewell, working together to put on events for the enjoyment of the city centre community is 'one of many examples of friendship and co-operation between the church and the City Council'. The square is often used for dance groups, choirs and community singing. Local theatre groups also use it to preview productions to help generate publicity. Dancing grannies on motorised shopping trolleys were a recent act which the church's website says 'brought Oxford to a standstill and our minister

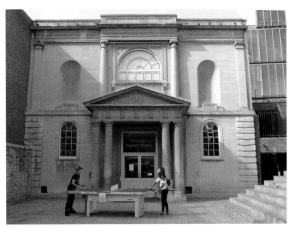

Exterior before the opening up of Bonn Square, June 2007. PHOTO JW

Table tennis in front of the church, August 2013. PHOTO BP

New ceiling and lights of the chapel, January 2013. PHOTO NEW ROAD BAPTIST CHURCH

Top Ecumenical celebration with donkey, Easter 2011.
PHOTO NICK PARSONS

Centre Escape to Safety, October 2010. PHOTO NICK PARSONS

Bottom Sacrificial event, August 2010. PHOTO NICK PARSONS

was most honoured to offer her office as a dressing-room for the grannies to put on their extensive make-up!'

For local groups there is a small charge on a sliding scale depending on the size of event. About ten days a year, they allow a commercial activity which brings more money for both the council and the church, but they always stipulate that it must have some community engagement.

Importantly, the chapel doors are open as much as possible. A group of people have committed to welcoming visitors to the building on Mondays to Fridays from 11am to 2pm. About 200 people come in during an average week. Kat Bracewell says that 'people come in with a variety of needs. Some come in regularly and there is a little mini-community here and others come in because they see the doors open and they are in "desperate extremis" and they want to talk with you and pray with you and that is an important part of what we can provide as well.'

CHALLENGE
We work hard to develop activities that we can put on in the square that will engage people and get them thinking about issues. It's always productive to have something practical that people can do, as it is a good way to start conversations.

WEBSITE
http://www.newroadbaptistchurchoxford.co.uk/

St Luke, Oxford

I think in an area where there is a lot of deprivation, it is important to give people a really top-quality building. The Revd Jane Sherwood

St Luke's Canning Crescent (as it is always known) is an unlisted church founded in 1933 as a mission hall for the area of Cold Harbour, in South Oxford. Canon Stather-Hunt, then vicar of St Matthew's Church on Marlborough Road, led the vision and the money was raised by the parish with the involvement of local council tenants.

The building is licensed for worship, but not consecrated, so it comes under the secular planning system rather than the Faculty Jurisdiction. As it is the daughter church of St Matthew's, it is St Matthew's PCC that has had the legal authority to apply for planning permission and put the works out to contract.

THE PROJECT

In 2009 The Big Project was launched to rebuild and renew the church. The design is based on the existing foundations, although extended slightly, and an additional room, the 'Chill-Out Room', is being added. The timber frame was in good condition so it will be retained, while the asbestos panelling and rotten woodwork are being removed.

Facilities include a new, fully equipped kitchen, better disabled access, increased office space and additional storage. The building is fully insulated. Works started in February 2013, and by the middle of November the same year the new church and community centre were fully functioning.

As evidence of their long-term commitment to the community, the PCC has negotiated a lease of 125 years, increased from five years, and a lower rent with the council, which owns the land.

REALISATION

St Luke's is in one of the poorest parts of the City of Oxford and it is the only community facility in the area. It has a long history of reaching out to the community. In the spring of 2013 it acted as an 'Ark' for nearby residents who were flooded out.

The Big Project's appeal strapline was: 'St Luke's exists to build community in the local area, and to bring spiritual inspiration, emotional support and practical help to those in need.' It already runs many regular activities, such as a baby and toddler group, a Monday Club for five- to eight-year-olds, Monday Plus for nine- to twelve-year-olds, Wednesday drop-in sessions for mainly older people, and Youth Space, an evening youth group for thirteen- to eighteen-year-olds. Jane Sherwood says: 'St Luke's is a church and a community centre and people who may not come on Sunday will come to one of our groups. A lot of our contact with the community is through our children's and young people's groups and family events.'

Andrew Smith, Chair of the Project Steering Group, says: 'There is a sense of ownership on the part of the neighbours. At one of our events, a member of one of the key local families said: "I've seen my kids come up through the Sunday School and I know I never come, but I still think of it as my church."'

It was open every day, but the building was deteriorating and becoming overcrowded. 'Previously,' says Jane Sherwood, 'everything happened in one big space. So someone could have been kicking a ball around while someone else was trying to work.'

The project has emerged from eight years of planning and careful consultation with the local community. The overall objective is to improve the quality of what is on offer. Those who need a quieter space will be able to use the Chill-Out Room for small group activities or one-to-one support. Properly equipped with IT, it will enhance St Luke's work with young and vulnerable people, for example helping them write CVs and look for jobs. The improved kitchen will encourage new skills, particularly in young people who love to cook. The building will be more accessible to disabled people. Ms Sherwood says that 'the presence of a really good community resource will also give value to people in the area, many of whom suffer low self-esteem and the effects of marginalisation. The increased meeting space will encourage more people to access the groups on offer, and reduce social isolation and loneliness.'

The PCC set up a steering committee of people with a wide range of experience, some among them previously involved in a major building project at St Matthew's. It found someone familiar with writing business plans, and a former professional charity fund-raiser.

From the start, local young people have been strongly involved in the design and fund-raising initiatives. It was the church's Youth Group that came up with the name The Big Project, which inspired everyone to aim high. Several of its members attended the early meetings with the architect, Stephen Wolstenholme of Stanhope Wilkinson Associates, and took part in the discussions about the design of the building and the activities envisaged. Jane Sherwood explains that their two priorities were 'the Chill-Out Room, which we are having added specifically with young people in mind, although all ages will use it, and a better-equipped kitchen'.

In 2010, members of the Youth Group put together a presentation for a Youth Capital Fund panel and succeeded in winning a £50,000 grant. Ms Sherwood says, 'This was a really positive achievement for them, some of whom have trouble at school, and the money has been put towards the Chill-Out Room. This kick-started our appeal back in 2010 really, and attracted other funding.'

The Steering Committee managed to raise the required £500,000 a few months after the building works started in February 2013. This left them with a further £50,000 to find for furniture and equipment, plus start-up costs for new youth and community projects.

The two biggest funders were WREN (£75,000) and Veolia Environmental Trust (£100,000); they also obtained funding from the Garfield Weston Foundation and other local charities. The Committee set up the 100 Club Scheme, in which people signed up to give a small amount each month for three years. This helped secure a loan from the Diocese to help with cash-flow.

There have been some imaginative fund-raising events. To emphasise that the fund-raising target had nearly been reached, the 2012 Pigs Can Fly summer fête had a pig theme, with a hog roast, a mini-'Olympigs' and the grand opening of a giant piggy bank made by the children. The Paintathon in September 2012 was a day when artists (including the vicar) painted all day and there were art workshops for all ages. The Youth Group has organised other events such as the annual St Luke's Got Talent contest, and cake sales, which have promoted the project within the community.

Everyone in the local community was invited to the last service and community lunch at St Luke's before the site handover, with the church specially decorated by a local artist with a 'tree of life' theme. The local Salvation Army Band then led a parade from St Luke's to the former site of South Oxford Baptist Church, where joint church services were held with the Salvation Army. The committee could rent space there, so all the midweek activities could continue. Since the end of November 2013 the congregation has been using the new church, but the committee is also looking for ways to continue the link with the Salvation Army.

The committee has worked to keep the project in the public eye and the local paper, the *Oxford Mail*, has published several articles. The committee has also produced a regular newsletter and posted updates and photographs of the ongoing works on the website.

Jane Sherwood says they want to continue the existing groups and look at working with other organisations to offer support to those dealing with

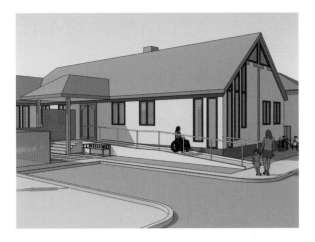

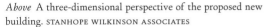

Above A three-dimensional perspective of the proposed new building. STANHOPE WILKINSON ASSOCIATES

Top right 'Pigs can fly' in front of the original building, June 2012. PHOTO JANE SHERWOOD

Right The 'El Salvador' cross designed by the Revd Jane Sherwood and painted by the children of St Luke's for Easter 2012 being carried into the new building, October 2013. PHOTO JANE SHERWOOD

Below The new church and community centre on completion, November 2013. PHOTO JW

The 'El Salvador' cross now hangs at the south end of the new church, November 2013. PHOTO JW

The new kitchen and craft sink for the Chill-Out Room, November 2013. PHOTO JW

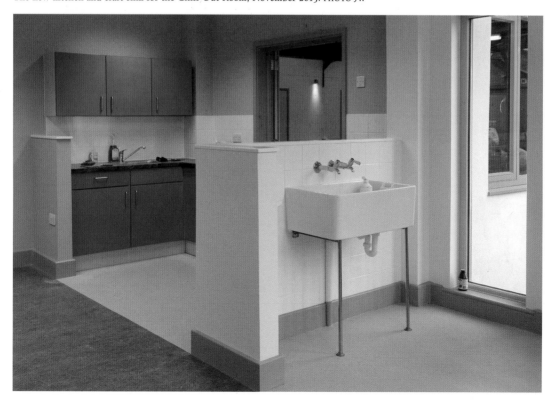

Two girls (on left) made the successful application to the Youth Capital Fund. The cake, in the shape of the new building, was raffled to raise more funds, November 2011.
PHOTO REVD JANE SHERWOOD

Detail from the Big Project appeal leaflet, 2012.
PHOTO BRIDGE BUILDER TRUST

debt and family break-ups. They want to run more courses in IT and help to support people back into employment. They already share a children/family worker and a youth worker with St Matthew's and help to raise funds to pay for the posts.

During the summer of 2013 the committee organised a survey of the 400 households in the parish to find out what activities they would like to see happening in the new church building. They hope that the better insulated and more energy-efficient building will reduce bills. Having two rooms will increase the potential for hiring out space, but this will have to be balanced against the space and time that this very active church will need for its own activities.

CHALLENGES

Getting planning permission for a building on a flood plain, negotiating a new lease with the council and fund-raising were all major challenges. But maybe the most emotional challenge was getting everyone to agree on a colour scheme. There were so many contradictory demands (vibrant/calming) that in the end the Steering Committee, while taking into account all these ideas, had to make some executive decisions.

BEST PIECE OF ADVICE

Hold on to your original vision, but be prepared to revise some of your plans. The first planning application was turned down and they had to submit several amended versions before obtaining approval. Andrew Smith says, rather than feeling discouraged, 'see it as a way of refining your project. Some of the grand ideas that we had to begin with, such as incorporating flats to raise income through letting out parts of the building, turned out not to be what the neighbourhood wanted. They wanted a proper successor to the old St Luke's and so that is what we have created.'

WEBSITE

http://www.stlukesoxford.org.uk/

St Michael at the North Gate, Oxford

I think of St Michael's as a Christian community, with a civic calling and a city centre opportunity. The Very Revd Bob Wilkes, City Rector and Priest-in-Charge

St Michael's is situated on the pedestrianised Cornmarket Street, one of the busiest shopping streets in Oxford. The bustling university city is estimated to attract 9.5 million visitors a year and inevitably many of them walk past St Michael's during their stay. The AMT coffee stand and seating beside the south entrance only add to the constant throng of people outside the building.

This Grade I listed church, originally situated just within the North Gate of the city, is one of the oldest buildings in Oxford. The present church tower, built of coral ragstone in about 1050, is the only surviving part of the original Saxon church. It was rebuilt in the thirteenth century and altered and enlarged in the fourteenth and fifteenth centuries. The church was substantially restored and the chancel rebuilt in 1854 by G. E. Street.

THE PROJECT

A parish centre was built at the rear of the church in the 1970s and a visitors' centre added to the north porch in the early 1980s. More recently, a new sound system was installed in 2011 and a sophisticated new lighting system and internal decoration followed in 2012.

The PCC is developing plans to improve the main, south entrance leading off Ship Street, which has heavy oak doors, usually kept closed to conserve heat. It would like to replace the inner pair of doors with glass ones so that the inside of the church is more visible on the approach into the porch, making that area brighter and more welcoming to everyone. It is also close to agreeing plans for a re-landscaping of the 'AMT' corner.

REALISATION

When the Very Revd Bob Wilkes was appointed City Rector in 2009, he felt his first job was to clarify the purpose of St Michael's and what 'it was there for'.

First and foremost, he says, it is the worshipping home for a Christian community from all over the city. St Michael's does not have a residential parish. People come for the traditional style of worship and the high quality of the professional music.

Secondly, St Michael's is Oxford's City Church and most civic religious services are held there. Mr Wilkes is the City Rector for Oxford appointed by the City Council and has his own seat in the Council Chamber. The front row of pews has a decorative stand that holds the Lord Mayor's Mace when he or she is attending a service.

Its third role comes out of what Bob Wilkes describes as 'the city centre opportunity which is something we are given every day of the week'. He says that the first act in St Michael's city centre mission 'is to open the door of the church every day from 10am to 5pm and offer a space in which to step aside and enjoy the quiet'. There is now a clearly identifiable prayer corner by the font, which is appreciated, as shown by the number of prayer requests recorded every week in the prayer book provided, often filling several pages.

With the oldest church tower in Oxford, the church is a tourist landmark, and offers visitors the opportunity to climb the tower, which gives a panoramic view of the city and the hills beyond. They can also view the Treasury on the first floor, with its collection of artefacts and relics from the church's history. The tower receives 12,000 visitors every year.

Public access to the tower was initiated in the late 1980s. In the early 1990s, a glass Visitor Reception Centre was added to the north porch to provide a separate entrance to the tower, and is the entrance most used by visitors. By charging for tower admissions the church can afford a full-time manager, who provides a welcome for visitors and offers the basic security cover that enables the building to open daily.

Several steps have been taken to improve the way visitors experience the church: marketing specialists were hired to produce new communication materials; interpretative notices, pull-up banners and leaflets offer welcome and helpful information. To express the building's various roles, the strap-lines *City:Church, City:Worship, City:Music* and *City:Thinking* were created and are used throughout all its materials.

A further opportunity for promoting St Michael's came in 2012, when the same marketing team worked for Churches Together in Central Oxford to produce the leaflet *Discover Churches in Oxford*. St Michael's website has also been improved and is now regularly updated.

Music is very important as another way of bringing people into the church and the building works well acoustically for small-scale musical events. There is a free Monday lunchtime concert provided by musicians who perform for nothing, with a collection taken for a charity nominated by the performers. In 2012, performances averaged seventy-five attendees, some regulars, others passers-by. There is no shortage of musicians wanting performance space and musical groups also hire the church for their own performances. Mr Wilkes says they are 'fortunate to have St Michael's and All Saints Charities, a Trust that enables them to employ a paid director of music and semi-professional singers so when we turn out a musical service it is top quality'.

Over the last three summers, it has offered a series of Sunday afternoon Bach Cantata choral evensongs with regular church members acting as hosts. These are followed by a free cream tea and are attended by, on average, seventy-five people, most of whom are visitors to Oxford. Mr Wilkes says they chose evensong deliberately as 'tradition looks like

The Saxon tower on busy Cornmarket Street, July 2013. PHOTO JW

South entrance and AMT café stand and seating off Ship Street, August 2013. PHOTO BP

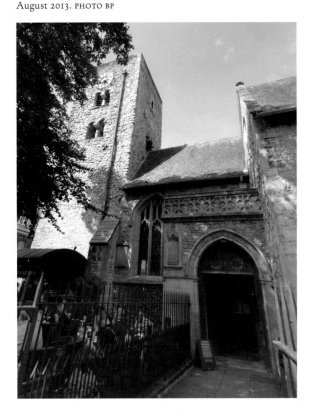

Oxford and a choral evensong fits and for someone who is not very familiar with what goes on in church, choral evensong can be a very easy service to attend'.

A new venture was the development of the City Thinking Forum at the end of 2012. This aims to have a led debate on a current social issue, with the emphasis on local application. The first theme, in November 2012, was 'The living wage' and for January 2013 it was 'Affordable housing'. The debates are held post-work and include a glass of wine. Initial feedback has encouraged the organisers to develop the programme. Recently, a programme of Public Theology debates has been added at lunchtimes.

An important way in which St Michael's engages with city-centre life is by offering its central facilities to groups doing good social work within the city.

In the 1970s a Parish Room was built to the north-east of the church, reached via a passageway running along the north side. Since 2013, the basement has housed a popular Fair Trade shop, which is run as a social enterprise and is a tenant of the church. The Parish Room is hired out to groups such as AA, Samaritans, U3A, Cruse, Fellow English classes, Oasis, Oxford Centre for Spiritual Growth and many other groups. The room is recognised as a valuable resource and the PCC is making plans to refurbish and refurnish it completely to provide a more usable and pleasant space for such groups to meet.

Support from the St Michael's and All Saints Charities, established specifically to support the church, means it can afford to pay for staff to undertake the public ministry involved in being a city-centre church and to develop the musical aspect of its outreach work. These charities have responsibility for maintaining the fabric of the building within their terms. The new lighting system and redecoration were carried out in 2012 at a cost of £90,000, two thirds of which came from the Charities and one third from the congregation.

CHALLENGES

If you are ministering to passers-by, they will pass by and you are constantly reaching out to new people. Much of the weekday outreach work is undertaken by the staff team. The challenge is to find a way to build bridges between the congregational life and the city mission, much of which is staff-led.

WEBSITE

http://www.smng.org.uk/

Below View of the west end, the staircase and balcony up to the tower and first-floor Treasury and the Visitors' Centre at the north entrance, August 2013. PHOTO BP

Bottom Close-up of the entrance to the Visitors' Centre, July 2013. PHOTO JW

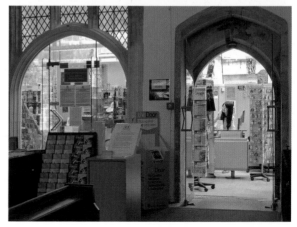

St John the Baptist, Stadhampton

I think that the church and the village hall are the heart of a village. If these two are combined, then you have a win-win situation. A response to the consultation undertaken in the village between December 2008 and February 2009

Stadhampton is a village of about 800 people five miles north of Wallingford in South Oxfordshire. The small church of St John the Baptist is on the northern edge beside the village green, which is surrounded by some of the oldest houses, but is now bisected by the B480.

The Grade II listed church has stood on its present site since the twelfth century, but the present building dates from 1588. It was restored and enlarged by E. G. Bruton in 1875. The other church in the benefice, St Katherine, Chiselhampton, is already closed and being looked after by the Churches Conservation Trust.

THE PROJECT

The Stadhampton Community Building Project wanted to create a village hall within the church to provide the residents with an 'aesthetically pleasing, practical and accessible place to meet'. Services and telecommunication cables had to be brought in. A small extension was added to the west end of the south aisle to house the new boiler and the toilets, one fully accessible. A kitchen was installed at the west end of the north aisle. The floor was replaced and underfloor heating installed. The pews were replaced by new chairs. A new lighting system is in place, and fund-raising is continuing for a new audio-visual system, including a drop-down screen that will serve equally well for a film club and family services. The church was redecorated throughout. Works commenced on site on 1 March 2013 and the building reopened in October 2013. While works were ongoing, the church was able to use the school hall and St Katherine's to hold services.

REALISATION

The vision for the project was defined as 'not just about bricks and mortar; we aim to build a caring and cohesive community and to do that we need a community building'. It was very definitely a joint community and church initiative. The church does not have its own website, and information about it is an intrinsic part of the Stadhampton community website.

Stadhampton has not had a village hall since the 1960s when the old hall was demolished. There is a school hall, but its use is limited to evenings and weekends and, as the school continues to grow, it has become less practical to hire it out.

The church, although beside the village green, is quite isolated and the building was damp and cold. Although basically in good repair, it did not have any mains water or drainage, and stood empty for six days a week. The PCC was, therefore, delighted to be approached by the Building Project Team to discuss the possibility of a joint venture. Recognising the diminishing numbers in the congregation, the PCC realised that raising the church's profile by finding ways for it to be used in the service of the community was essential if it was to have a sustainable future. Two representatives from the PCC and the then vicar joined the Project Team.

A thorough consultation was carried out between December 2008 and February 2009. Approximately sixty-five families were interviewed face-to-face. A questionnaire was sent with the parish magazine to each of the 400 households and twenty were completed. This made a total response of eighty-five households, representing the views of 201 people

(25% of the population of Stadhampton and its environs). There followed an open meeting reporting on the findings of the consultation, which revealed that 89% of respondents wanted a village hall. There was a great deal of discussion about the two possible options identified: either building a new hall on the 'Pavilion' site or adapting the church. The 'Pavilion' site was acknowledged to be isolated, away from the centre of the village, and it was felt that the costs of a new build would be prohibitive. Importantly, it was recognised that modifying the church would also help preserve a much-loved historic building which 'had been at the heart of the community for over 900 years'. A report of the meeting appeared in the June 2009 parish magazine to ensure all households were informed of the decision. Further feedback was invited, and this openness has continued throughout the project.

Regular updates were published in the parish magazine; drawings, plans and proposed designs of the new lighting system and the chairs were on display at various village events and were permanently displayed in the church. The Building Project Team made regular reports to both the Parish Council and the Parochial Parish Council. When it became clear that the biggest concerns were about secular activities in a church and the times the hall would be used, another open meeting was held in October 2010. The experiences of other similar successful projects were described and it was agreed that a Hiring Agreement would be clearly worded to ensure that 'only appropriate activities would take place'.

The consultation process provided the opportunity to ask for volunteers to offer their time and expertise in various aspects of the project. Letters of support were requested from groups interested in using the proposed space, and these provided additional evidence for grant applications.

The estimated cost of the project was £380,000. The PCC organised many local fund-raising events, which increased community awareness. The Charity Ball at the Crazy Bear pub on the other side of the green from the church raised the most money, while the hog roast on the green was the best-attended. Funds were also raised by auctioning off the standard

nineteenth-century pine pews. The incumbent, the Revd Caroline King, estimates that about 80% have remained within the village.

Major grants were awarded by South Oxfordshire District Council's Community Investment Fund, WREN, Oxfordshire County Council's Big Society Fund, Biffa Awards, Stadhampton Parish Council and the South East LEADER Programme.

One of the major hurdles was the possible need for a formal agreement between all the key stakeholders to protect various interests. The Parish Council was concerned that if the church ever became redundant, some guarantee would be required that it would not be sold and that the new 'village hall' would continue to be available for community use. Additionally, the Funding Agreement issued by SODC for their grant of £100,000 included a claw-back clause stating that if the building were 'not available for community use, the Council may seek to recover all or a part of the grant already paid to the grant recipient'. This liability caused the members of the PCC considerable angst and legal advice was sought, at some expense. This meant a significant delay before the agreement could be signed as lawyers from the District Council entered into lengthy discussions with the Diocese.

The situation was ultimately resolved quite simply by two letters to the Parish Council. The first, from the PCC, outlined the members' commitment to the project; their desire to see the church continuing for both worship and as a village hall for many years to come; and their eagerness to work in partnership with the Parish Council in the ongoing management of the new facility. It also explained the Church of England's policy on closing churches. The second letter, from the Team Rector, reinforced support for the project. It explained the Church's redundancy policy in more detail and the statutory requirement to consult with the local community if redundancy were ever to be considered under the Pastoral Measure (1983). As a result, no other formal agreements were deemed necessary and SODC's Funding Agreement was eventually signed without the claw-back clause being amended.

The architects, Wallingford Architecture Ltd, and the Building Project Team set out to provide the

Above Exterior from the south-east. The completed new extension at the west end can just be seen at left, September 2013. PHOTO MIKE PECKETT

Right Interior before works done, looking towards the east end showing pews and Victorian tiles, December 2011. PHOTO JW

most practical, efficient and sustainable solutions
to all aspects of the project. The extension is fully
insulated and the need to clean and preserve the
roof timbers allowed the nave and aisle roofs to be
insulated as well, reducing heating costs. Thought
was given to the long-term future of the building's
fabric, and the new floor, laid throughout, is made
of 'Limecrete' mix which will allow it to breathe and
reduce the recurrence of damp. Outside, in order to
provide for increased and sustainable car parking, the
long driveway up to the church is to be improved and
proposals to upgrade the section of green adjacent to
the churchyard are currently being discussed with
the Parish Council.

Aesthetics have been important. The extension
has been designed to match the stonework and
windows of the church building. Likewise, the arched
doorway into the extension matches other doorways
in the church. Two types of oak chairs were ordered
from Irish Contract Seating, some solid oak with
beige seats to match existing stonework and new
limestone floor tiles, others of similar oak but with
a stackable metal frame. The kitchen units, sourced
from a local merchant, are screened off from the nave
and aisle by a timber enclosure with detail matching
the church's existing woodwork.

The church reopened on 13 October 2013 with
a Service of Celebration led by Bishop Colin,
and services resumed their normal pattern. The
opening weekend generated a great deal of interest
in holding concerts, morning coffee, quizzes, arts
and craft sessions and, said Ann Stead, Chair of
the Stadhampton Community Building Project
Committee, 'Enquiries came in to the new booking
clerk thick and fast. Within a few days, bookings had
been taken for three parties, two Christmas parties
and two charity fund-raisers and three people had
offered to organise a New Year's Eve Party for the
village.' Straight away, Pilates classes started on
Tuesday and Thursday mornings, followed later by
an evening class. A parent and toddler group started
in late October and has proved very successful. Plans
are afoot for a gardening club and a youth group to
start in January 2014 and an older people's lunch club
in February. The need for a film club was identified
very early in the consultation, so fund-raising is

Underfloor heating being laid in the nave, June 2013.
PHOTO MIKE PECKETT

The church during building work, looking towards the east end,
July 2013. PHOTO BP

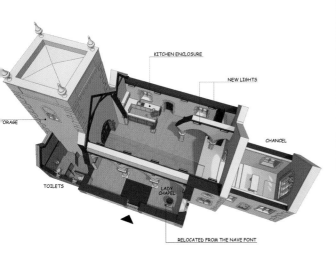

Cut-away perspective showing new toilet extension and position of kitchen, 2013. PHOTO WALLINGFORD ARCHITECTURE LTD

The completed kitchen at the west end of the north aisle, September 2013. PHOTO MIKE PECKETT

A consultation meeting, April 2009. PHOTO ANN STEAD

A mock-up showing an exercise class taking place in the refurbished building, January 2012. PHOTO DR NICKY PEET

The completed nave and chancel with the new chairs and the font in the south aisle, September 2013. PHOTO MIKE PECKETT

continuing for an audio-visual system that will enable films to be shown.

The PCC is getting used to a different way of using the building and is working to ensure the balance is right between its use as a village hall and as a continuing place of worship. An interim management committee has been formed to manage the day-to-day issues and give time to work out the details of how the partnership model of management will operate.

CHALLENGE
The decision to consult fully and on all aspects of the project throughout its duration was a major undertaking, but it ensured that concerns could be raised, discussed and resolved.

LESSONS LEARNED
When fund-raising locally, concentrate on organising productive activities. Do not exhaust your team by having to run too many events for small returns.

BEST PIECES OF ADVICE
Gather the evidence on the need and support for your project and constantly refine it. Funding bodies will expect to see such evidence. Work closely with grant officers. Build relationships with the Parish Council, District Council and County Council through your local councillors and MP. Continue to keep them informed.

Take photographs of events and changes made to the church as part of the project and create an archive. It is all part of the continuing history of the church.

It is important to provide a clear and consistent project brief, enabling consultants and builders to undertake the work and deliver the final product on time and on budget.

WEBSITE
Stadhampton community website: http://www.stadhampton.com/

St John the Evangelist, Stoke Row

We had had this light-bulb moment, when the Headmaster, Steve McTegart, said: 'If the school were able to get hold of grants to pay for the work in the church would we be able to use it as our hall?' The Revd Kevin Davies, Rector of Langtree Benefice

Stoke Row is at one of the highest points of the southern Chiltern Hills. With a population of 650, the village is little more than a main street. The church is at the west end. The pub and the independent chapel are at the east end, with the one shop in the centre.

The small Grade II listed church was built in 1846 by R. C. Hussey in thirteenth-century style, with knapped flint and stone dressings. The chancel is one eighth the length of the nave, separated by the communion rail; the altar is raised on a step. A tower at the north-east corner houses the vestry, clock and bell. One of the most significant features is the east rose window, designed and made in 1954 by Barbara Batt, who cut each of the 1,226 pieces of glass.

THE PROJECT

In December 2011, a wooden sprung floor with underfloor heating was laid on top of the original floor. The pews were removed and replaced with wood and fabric chairs. The neighbouring Church of England primary school now makes use of the building from Monday to Thursday during term-time.

REALISATION

The Stoke Row Primary School was founded in 1853 next door to the church, with which it has always been closely connected. A chance conversation between the Rector, the Revd Kevin Davies, and the former headteacher, Steve McTegart, has made that relationship even closer.

The school numbers had doubled since 2002 from fifty to almost a hundred and they needed a hall. Building a new hall on school grounds would have involved prohibitive costs and meant losing their only green space.

Coincidentally, since 2005 the PCC had been thinking about how it could create a more user-friendly, flexible space. Initial thoughts centred on developing a base for Reading church groups to come and use for a quiet day, where alternative worship could be practised. However, the PCC had found that removing the pews was going to cost about £100,000, a very large sum for a small PCC and congregation.

In 2007, the Revd Kevin Davies and Steve McTegart were talking after a school assembly in the church building, and Mr Davies asked, 'How big a space do you need?' Mr McTegart replied, 'Well, a space like this.' He went on to ask about obtaining grants. From there a partnership was born.

The school had specific requirements that had to be built into the design. It needed a sprung wooden floor for gym and games. Rigorous standards of health and safety had to be met in terms of additional fixtures and fittings, such as fire alarms and smoke detectors.

The school was in the process of becoming a church school and moving from Voluntary Control to Voluntary Aided, which meant that it was able to access capital funds from the Diocese's Board of Education. So it paid entirely for this initial phase of work, which cost just under £80,000.

The school and church undertook a consultation process to show that there was support for the project. It was publicised in the village magazine, and questionnaires were sent out. Parents were encouraged to write to the Diocesan Chancellor to tell him 'what a brilliant idea this was and how important it was and how much the facility was needed'. This formed a part of the evidence needed for planning permission and a faculty.

Kevin Davies says that 'there were about three vitriolic letters, but overall there was fairly overwhelming support for it'.

The school uses the building for four days a week under licence. Mr Davies explains, 'The building is theirs from Mondays to Thursdays inclusive during term-time in school hours. If they want to do something after school on one of their days they can, and if we want to do something after school on one of their days we have to ask, but it is a very relaxed arrangement. They can use it on Fridays, but we have first call.' It has not so far proved a problem, even for funerals, as in a small village there are likely to be only three or so a year.

The school pays an annual rent and contributes to the insurance and utility costs. A user agreement was drawn up setting out what the school can and cannot do. Basically, it can do almost anything, says Kevin Davies, 'apart from non-Christian worship, holding séances, drinking alcohol or running a disco'. Anything unusual is checked with the church in advance. The school uses it for the daily worship service and special events such as carol services. Otherwise, it is used for games, music and PE as well as other activities involving large groups.

Kevin Davies adds, 'Now it is a church school, we have a greater representation on the governing body and a lovely sense of commitment and involvement, and they know they are welcome to come and make full use of our building.'

The small congregation of between six and twelve people meets for a weekly Sunday service. To replace the pews the PCC bought forty large comfortable chairs. Part of the cost was raised by selling off some of the pews, but others, sadly, were damaged when removed. Most chairs can be stacked in cupboards at the back, which were put in at the same time as the work on the floor was done. The rest can go up in the sanctuary area during the week and come out again for Sunday and other services.

It was not felt necessary to create any more of a distinction between the chancel, the 'sacred space', and the nave, the part used by the school, than that already provided by the communion rail. Likewise, Kevin Davies says, 'It would have been a step too far to turn it into just a hall, and we would probably not have got the unanimity that we got from the PCC and the members of the congregation if we had cleared everything out.' The altar, pulpit and font are all still at the east end.

The PCC is now fund-raising for a second phase of work, an extension to the church to house a fully accessible toilet and kitchenette, so that, Mr Davies says, 'we can complete our vision of offering hospitality'. Planning permission has already been granted and it is hoped to be able to complete the work by spring 2014. The current estimates are between £120,000 and £140,000. They have recently been awarded a grant from South Oxfordshire District Council and are currently applying for Lottery money. Mr Davies adds, 'Now that we have got the school within the building we've got demonstrable community use already and that opens up the possibility of Big Lottery Funding and things like that.'

Kevin Davies is sure that this project has now turned the building into a place with a future. 'It was pretty clear to me on moving into this team ministry that for Stoke Row Church to have a future it needed to do something other than merely Sunday worship.'

Daphne Stallwood, who was married in the church and has been churchwarden for the past thirteen years, said: 'It gives everyone a flexible space to enjoy and there are all sorts of possibilities open to us.'

The PCC is now developing its vision for expanding and building the community around the church, using its existing networks. The school has a sharing assembly on Friday mornings in the church that parents are starting to attend. Once the toilet and kitchenette are built, the PCC is hoping to organise a coffee morning for parents after the sharing assembly.

CHALLENGES

For this project, the PCC not only had to obtain permissions, but also had to arrange a licence between the church and the school's governing body. Negotiations between Local Education Authority lawyers and diocesan lawyers took a

Exterior from the east, June 2013. PHOTO JW

long time and the PCC nearly lost the grant from the other part of the Diocese, the Diocesan Board of Education.

One person was needed on the PCC who could concentrate on the administration and remain on top of the legal side so that others could concentrate on the fund-raising.

BEST PIECE OF ADVICE

Plan for the long haul and do not think it can be done in two years. You might raise the money in two years, but it's a juggling act to have the money in place and obtain the necessary permissions. For Phase 2 of this project, Stoke Row was awarded a grant from SODC, but had to have the faculty reviewed because it had expired.

WEBSITE

http://www.langtree.org/stoke_row.htm

Interior before works done, showing the pews and original floor, September 2004. PHOTO JW

The school using the church during Maths Week, July 2013, after the pews were removed and a new floor laid. The tent is a giant function machine and the two members of staff are dressed as scientists. PHOTO STOKE ROW SCHOOL

St Mary and St Edburga, Stratton Audley

*The challenge is to use our churches or lose them. But I can hear the cry go up –
'They are too cold to be used, there is no toilet and no running water etc.' I agree,
but there could be, if only people were encouraged to take an interest in their church
buildings before it is too late.* The Rector, the Revd Christobel Hargraves, in the July 2013 Benefice
magazine, *The Shelswell News*

Stratton Audley is a small village two and a
half miles north-east of Bicester in north-east
Oxfordshire, with about 150 dwellings and 360
adults. The church is at the centre of the village.
There is one pub and no village hall.

The Grade 1 listed church dates from the twelfth
century but was largely rebuilt in the thirteenth and
fourteenth centuries. In 1861 the church was fully
restored, at the cost of £800, by the architect Roger
Smith. This entailed removing the chancel screen, re-
laying the floor and installing new pews in both nave
and aisles.

THE PROJECT

In 2007, following extensive fund-raising over the
previous eight years to cover major repairs to the
fabric, the £9,000 remaining was used to create a
toilet and a tea point at the west end of the church,
either side of the tower. Between September and
December 2009, the centre pews were removed
and replaced by new oak chairs. The Victorian tile
paving in the side aisles was taken up and reused. A
reinforced floor was laid in the central area, overlaid
with insulation slabs, and the Victorian central
heating duct retained. Underfloor central heating
pipes were fitted in the central area, overlaid with
limestone floor tiles.

REALISATION

St Mary and St Edburga's is part of the Shelswell
Benefice, formed of ten parishes, all of whose parish
churches are listed but which has a total population
of less than 2,500. The Rector, the Revd Christobel
Hargraves, has challenged her PCCs to think about
how they can ensure that the assets the buildings
represent are put to good use so that they survive
into the next century. She says, 'While they are
special places set aside to worship God, they are of
much more importance to our communities than they
seem at face value. I understand that some people
do not wish to worship in church, but I am equally
aware that there are people who would be devastated
if the heritage represented in our beautiful church
buildings was lost.'

St Mary and St Edburga's PCC has taken up this
challenge. In 2006, faced with nave pews that needed
major repairs, it starting thinking about removing
them altogether. This would necessitate the laying
of a new floor, creating the opportunity to improve
the heating system and make a more flexible space for
worship, church activities and community use.

In July 2006 the DAC visited the church and
encouraged the PCC to proceed. English Heritage,
which had previously given a substantial grant
towards repairs, was consulted, together with
the local authority and the Victorian Society. No
objections were made. The central pews to be
removed were from the 1861 Victorian restoration,
and not of good quality, while the better pews in
the north and south aisles were to be retained. John
Beaumont, who played a major role in managing the
reordering project, explains that 'keeping the side
pews was partly about providing some continuity,
but also about being able to cater for large weddings
or funerals'.

An open village meeting was held in 2006, when
the outline of the proposals was explained. There was
considerable resistance, especially over the proposal

to remove the central pews. Dorothy Howarth, one of the churchwardens and a member of the Fabric Committee at the time, says that 'there was a fear that without the pews, it would not feel quite so much like church and some of the mysterious reverence would disappear'.

No one disagreed that the priority in making it a more welcoming church was the need for a toilet and basic kitchen facilities; this work was agreed at the open meeting and put in hand in 2007. The works cost about £9,000 and were funded from the remaining church fabric funds and local contributions. The kitchen, although not fully fitted, is versatile and has a facility for keeping food hot.

Water was already connected to the outside of the church but new drains were dug along the church paths (overseen by the Oxford Archaeological Unit) and water piped in for the tea point and toilets. Both the servery and the toilets have been cleverly tucked away, the former at the west end of the south aisle and the toilets in part of what was a very large vestry at the west end of the north aisle.

The villagers were invited to a second open meeting in November 2008 and the important proposal to remove the pews was again discussed. There was much less opposition this time, particularly when better-quality chairs were displayed.

The original estimate for the cost of the new scheme was £23,000 and an application was made to WREN, which offered a grant of £17,500. The PCC appointed Alan J. Frost as architect. A faculty was granted in May 2009 and work began in September that year.

Shortly afterwards the contractor, Roger N. Cross Services, suggested it would be much better to refloor a larger area of the church and at the same time to modernise the existing heating system, combining it with underfloor heating powered from the oil-fired boiler.

The PCC decided that the obsolete but decorative Victorian cast-iron heating grille should be retained as a reminder of the past, but covered by protective glass, to stop dirt dropping through it and to enable those wearing high heels to walk on it!

Following consultation with the Diocesan Registrar, it was sensibly agreed that these alterations could be added to the original faculty. It was found possible to tile an area of floor adjacent to the tea point that had been damaged by water following the theft of lead from the church roof, thereby utilising all the old clay tiles.

The work was completed in December 2009. Fifty stacking wooden chairs were purchased from a church in South London and fifty more comfortable oak chairs with burgundy upholstery were ordered from Irish Contract Seating, with the backrest incorporating a carved replica of the clover and poppy motifs found on the retained aisle pews.

The total cost of the scheme was £34,265. The cost of the new oak chairs, £7,972, was provided by individuals sponsoring the purchase of a chair or chairs, together with the relevant Gift Aid; the sale of the old pews covered the cost of the stacking chairs. Additional money came from an insurance payment, an existing fabric fund and reclaimed VAT from the Listed Places of Worship Grant Scheme. The fabric fund was augmented during the course of the work from an Open Gardens Weekend and scarecrow competition.

For John Beaumont, the overall benefit is that the church is now a much friendlier place. He says that the pews used to block the lower sections of the pillars and now there is much more of a feeling of space and openness, which 'is uplifting'.

The seating capacity is now greater and the chairs can be arranged to suit different forms of worship and church gatherings. John Beaumont describes how previously 'with a small congregation of between twenty and twenty-five, people wanted to sit in their own pew and usually at the back, which created huge gaps. No one intends to be unfriendly, but it has that effect and if you are taking the service, it is difficult to know where to look.'

The congregation has both formal services, where the chairs face the altar, and more informal services, at which they are placed so that people can face each other, bringing them together. The chairs can be moved to ensure that everyone can see everything going on rather than being blocked by a pillar. There is now more space for worshippers to congregate afterwards for tea and coffee, and to circulate and talk to each other.

Exterior from the south, October 2004. PHOTO JW

Interior before works done, with pews and purple carpet down the nave, October 2004. PHOTO JW

For Dorothy Howarth, the changes have allowed a different environment to be created, but on a personal level she does feel that some of the reverence has been lost. 'Some services feel like more of a Friendly Society type of meeting. It is not all to do with the reordering, and some of the more informal style has come from the introduction of new, more modern types of services.' Her reservations aside, she fully appreciates the good reasons for making the church more adaptable for use by a village with no other large community space. 'We were able to use the church for a wide variety of things prior to the pews coming out because it had a very wide centre aisle, and activities included jazz bands, theatrical productions, quizzes and Murder Mystery evenings, but the increased open space – which is brighter because of the light floor and with the benefit of the attractive and comfortable chairs – means that the church can be used more effectively.'

In addition to a continuation of the previous events, new activities have been introduced, including a regular singing group, which appreciates the wonderful acoustics, and a group that gets together regularly for short-mat bowls.

The village has an active social life, in which many activities are organised by the church, usually as part of the fund-raising efforts. Events include safari suppers, boules evenings, race nights, and jazz-in-the-garden dinners. Many of these events occur around the village in people's homes and gardens, but one course of the safari suppers is regularly taken in the church, and there are other concerts, exhibitions and banquets.

The Parish Council, while usually meeting in the pub, now uses the church for open public meetings. Meetings to develop the current Stratton Audley Community Plan are also held in the building. Dorothy Howarth says it is increasingly being acknowledged as an amenity for the whole village, but that they cannot become complacent as 'we have fewer children coming to the church than we used to and the building could still be used more'.

The job of continuing to look after the church goes on. In 2009 a loop and sound system was installed. A roof alarm has since been fitted which, it is known, has deterred other lead theft attempts. The next job is stonework repairs to the porch.

Looking to the future, the PCC invited local non-churchgoers to become Friends of the Church and to make a regular £5 contribution per month, gift-aided to the building's maintenance fund. John Beaumont says, 'It is quite usual to hear people say "I'm not an avid churchgoer but I think the building is part of our heritage and I would like to support that."'

CHALLENGES

The biggest challenge was deciding to refloor a larger area of the church and to modernise the existing heating system after the PCC had already obtained a faculty. Fortunately, the new works were allowed to be included within the existing permission.

BEST PIECES OF ADVICE

Spend time choosing the right kind of chair. They need to be of good quality, and comfortable because 'if people are coming to a wedding or a funeral, they don't want to feel they are coming into a canteen'.

Do not make the mistake of getting too many chairs or you will feel just as cluttered as before. One solution is to have a certain number of good solid chairs for regular use and another set of stackable ones that can be hidden away. Make sure the chairs are easy to lift, otherwise you won't have enough volunteers to do the moving!

WEBSITE

http://www.shelswellparishes.info/stratton.php

Top Interior after works done, looking towards the east end, two rows of the new chairs set out either side of the Victorian heating grille and the pews retained in the north and south aisles, July 2013. PHOTO BP

Above Village party in January 2010 to celebrate the completion of the reordering. PHOTO JOHN BEAUMONT

Right The servery at the west end of the south aisle, July 2013. PHOTO BP

St Nicholas, Tackley

A well designed and well crafted installation, which is sensitive to the architectural space around it, can enhance the beauty of the building. Sylvia Reddington, churchwarden

Tackley is a village of about 1,000 residents ten miles north of Oxford. It is a mixture of old cottages, converted buildings and new housing. There is a much-used village hall in the centre, which since 2004 has housed the seven-day-a-week community shop and the post office. The Grade II* listed parish church of St Nicholas stands in a prominent position on top of a hill at a slight distance from the village.

The church dates from the eleventh century but retains remnants of its original Saxon stonework. It is of cruciform shape with a central tower; the south aisle was added in the thirteenth century. The transepts were rebuilt in the fifteenth century and the north transept was again rebuilt in 1616 as a family chapel for John Harbourne. G. E. Street restored the church in 1864, adding a porch and new oak pews, pulpit, choir stalls and communion rails.

THE PROJECT

In December 2011, mains water was laid on and an octagonal pod containing a kitchenette and a fully accessible toilet was installed at the west end of the south aisle. The unused south porch was glazed in to provide a soundproof area for children. The following year the heating system was modernised.

REALISATION

In 2008, the church launched a £140,000 'Warmer Welcome Appeal', with the aim of making the building more welcoming and encouraging more people to make use of it as a community space. The project was managed by the Standing Committee of the PCC, which consisted largely of the Rector, the churchwardens and the treasurer. They set up a separate Appeals Committee, which came up with a lot of original ideas. They produced a well-designed appeal brochure, which went to everyone in the village and helped to attract funds. Fund-raising events were used to bring people into the church.

It took about three years to raise the money. Approximately £50,596 came from grants awarded by the All Churches Trust, the Garfield Weston Foundation, the Oxfordshire Historic Churches Trust, Viridor and the Doris Field Trust. VAT was claimed back under the Listed Places of Worship Grant Scheme. Donations and fund-raising events raised £71,704 while Gift Aid brought in a further £5,373.

The two most urgent practical tasks were to install mains water and update the 1930s heating system. Underfloor heating was considered, but it was thought too expensive to take up the floor, so the committee kept the oil-fired boiler, reclaimed some of the radiators and replaced others. This proved to be more expensive than originally estimated, as some of the longer pipes under the floor had to be replaced. The chancel and the nave can now be heated separately, which is useful as most of the normal Sunday services, having only a very small congregation, are held in the chancel.

A toilet was seen as essential for when the local school visited the building, and it 'would help to make some of the elderly congregation feel more secure'. A lot of time was spent trying to work out where the facilities should go: eventually the toilet and the servery were situated at the west end of the south aisle, which had been cold, damp and largely unused. The design breakthrough came

Top Exterior from the south-west, September 2006, showing the south aisle, whose roof was stripped of lead in February 2012.
PHOTO JW

Above Looking down the nave towards the chancel at the east end. The octagonal pulpit can be seen on the left, September 2006.
PHOTO JW

Right Glazed-in south porch from the south aisle, July 2013.
PHOTO BP

when architect Robert Mullan of Frame Architects Ltd suggested making the servery an octagonal pod to match the late-nineteenth-century eight-sided wooden pulpit. Room has been found for all the pews moved to accommodate the facilities – two are in the south porch and the rest in the south aisle.

These works had been completed for only two months when, on a Friday night in February 2012, thieves stripped the entire south aisle roof of lead just above the newly finished facilities. The crime was discovered the following morning by Sylvia Reddington, churchwarden, and Gill Withers, a local resident and fund-raising volunteer who had come to show representatives from Viridor the new work.

'There was rubble all over the floor. Fortunately, after a call for help, villagers rallied round and covered the damaged roof with tarpaulins just before heavy snow fell at midday, otherwise the new timber would have been ruined,' said Sylvia.

It took another year to get agreement and a faculty to replace the lead with terne metal-coated stainless steel. The insurance paid only part of the cost, and the church had to fund-raise and seek grants to make up the difference.

The pod, the toilet and the glazing-in of the south porch have made a big difference to the look of the interior. Churchgoers are enthusiastic about the design. As Sylvia says, 'We could so easily have had something very plain, but thanks to the architect, the pod we have – a lot of people say, and I think it is true – has actually beautified the church. It is very elegant and now looks as though it has always been there.'

The new facilities have made a big difference to those using the building. At a consultation meeting, a key concern was that a toilet would mean intrusive noise. In fact, it has proved to be 100% soundproof. The sides of the servery can be opened to provide two hatchways, one facing east and one north, and this means that serving coffee, tea and light refreshments after services and concerts is much easier. Having water and a toilet has also made a huge difference to the volunteers who come to do the flowers, clean the church and look after the churchyard, and the school is now using the church twice a term.

Ironically, now that the glazed-in, soundproof area has been created for children in the south porch, there are currently no children in the congregation and health and safety issues have been raised about using the space, which the committee is trying to resolve. It can be used as a break-out space for a crying child and mother. A future Sunday School may continue to meet in the south transept, where the organ, situated between transept and chancel, helps to contain any noise.

For the foreseeable future the PCC has decided to keep all the remaining pews, as they are still essential for school visits, large church festivals, weddings and funerals. Since the completion of the project the church has raised another £6,000 to re-gild the clock.

An immediate priority is to improve disabled access from the road into the church. Parking is difficult too: there is some space in a field behind the churchyard, but if that is full people have to walk up a fairly long, steep hill, which tends to limit the use of the church. Its beautiful setting means it is ideal for concerts, but possibly less suitable for weekly or more regular events.

Sylvia admits that she and the rest of the team need a rest: 'We had so much work over the actual appeal and all the extra work over the stolen lead, and we had organised quite a lot of concerts during that time.' There has twice been an interregnum during the life of the project, which added to the level of responsibility borne by the volunteers. A new incumbent was appointed in July 2013 and this is seen as an opportunity to start thinking about how to promote the church as a welcoming venue with a special ambience, well worth walking up the hill for.

A difficulty is the fact that the village hall is located right in the centre of the village, next to the school, playing fields, allotments and children's playground, so it is very well used by regular groups as well as for wedding receptions, parties and village events. Since 2004, it has housed the community shop.

Tackley is an active community, and over the last fourteen years there has been a succession of large village projects which have all required hard work by volunteers. Between 2000 and 2004, £425,000 was raised for the community shop and to upgrade the village hall. As described, between 2008 and

Looking down the south aisle towards the kitchen pod and toilet at the west end, July 2013. PHOTO BP

2011 the church raised £140,000 and the playground committee is currently fund-raising £90,000 to upgrade the children's playground. There is a danger of fund-raising fatigue unless new blood can be encouraged to get involved, but, on the positive side, the events are a good way of bringing the community together.

In 2011 the Parish Council, the Parochial Church Council, the Methodist Church and the village hall committee united to bid successfully – under the British Gas 'Green Streets' initiative – for funds to put solar panels on the roof of the village hall. Three roofs had originally been looked at, the village hall, the Methodist Church hall and St Nicholas, but the south-facing village hall roof had the biggest surface area. The energy generated helps light the village hall and shop and run the underfloor heating system. Of the income from selling surplus energy to the national grid, 72% goes to the village hall and shop, 20% to the church and 8% to the Methodist Church hall.

The church is obviously a valuable asset to Tackley, but it may well face difficulties in ensuring it is used to its full potential.

CHALLENGE

Finding expert help. The experience of a local resident, Gill Withers, who used to fund-raise in her professional life, was enormously helpful in completing complex application forms.

LESSONS LEARNED

Ensure you set up a good appeals committee. You need a range of skills and experience, including ideas people, fund-raisers, managers, people with links to other village organisations – and a sense of humour! Many members were from outside the church community.

BEST PIECE OF ADVICE

Ask the DAC for advice and support as early as possible.

WEBSITE

A good village website includes St Nicholas: http://www.tackleyvillage.co.uk/index.html

ST MARY THE VIRGIN, THAME

Without the reordering it would have been virtually impossible for us to have approached building the congregation up in the way that we wished to. The Revd Alan Garratt, Team Rector

Thame is an historic, busy market town eighteen miles east of Oxford, with a population of 11,200. St Mary's is in the north-west of the town just off the High Street. Its tower dominates the skyline.

The Grade 1 listed church is a large cruciform building dating from the early thirteenth century. The aisles and south porch were added in the fourteenth century, followed by the clerestory and the addition of two upper stages to the tower. The north and south transepts were reconstructed with new windows in the mid-fifteenth century. New open pews were installed in 1843 and the whole building was restored in 1889 by J. O. Scott.

THE PROJECT
Following two hearings of the Consistory Court, a major reordering and refurbishment took place between September and December 1991.

Nineteenth-century oak pews were removed and replaced by locally made ash chairs. A raised dais was built beneath the tower to accommodate a new nave table. The pulpit was moved from the north side of the tower arch to the south transept chapel and the font from the west end to the centre of the north aisle, facing the main south entrance. The floors in the nave and aisles were renewed with Welsh slate, replacing broken tiles and wood, and underfloor heating was installed. The nineteenth-century pipe organ was replaced by an electronic one and new lighting and sound systems introduced. The whole church was lime-washed by the traditional method.

REALISATION
The PCC and congregation had been discussing reordering since the mid-1980s. The Revd Chris Neal, who was very keen to be involved, became the incumbent in 1986. A discreet toilet and kitchen extension had been built off the north aisle in 1982, but restoration, repair and redecoration of the church's interior were becoming urgent. In particular, seating and floors at the north-west end were in a poor state where the nineteenth-century woodwork had rotted.

The main motivation was liturgical: the PCC wanted the layout of the church to reflect the way the growing congregation wished to worship. St Mary's has a very large chancel, about the same length as the nave, further separated from the congregation by the tower crossing. The view of the high altar is partly blocked by the large Lord Williams table tomb in the centre of the chancel.

Since the late 1970s an altar on the nave floor forward of the tower crossing had been used to create a more inclusive worship space, but, says Helena Fickling, now a churchwarden, 'It was all very shabby and just not glorious enough really for the worship of God. After the consecration at the nave altar, communion was actually administered from the high altar and everybody walked up through the chancel to receive it at the altar rail.'

The PCC wanted to facilitate the use of the building for additional community activities such as concerts, plays and exhibitions. As it was so close to the town centre there was huge potential, but 'completely pewed-out, it uses were limited'.

In 1987 Robert Maguire, one of three architects

Before the reordering. PHOTO JBKS ARCHITECTS

Exterior from the south, April 2009. PHOTO JW

Close-up of the nave altar and choir stalls behind, July 2013. PHOTO BP

interviewed, was commissioned to produce proposals to meet both these objectives.

The main challenge was to create a nave altar arrangement with altar rails so that the Eucharist would become the focus, visible to everyone. Robert Maguire designed a semicircular raised platform under the tower crossing, which projects out into the nave like an apron stage, reusing the original blue brick tiles of the nave floor. He proposed that the pulpit, on the pillar to the left looking towards the altar, which was felt to deflect from the communion, should move to the south transept. He also proposed to move the font from the west door to the north aisle and the north transept screen to the vestry partition.

The plans included the replacement of the poor-quality 1843 pews with chairs and the installation of an Allen Digital organ MDS 65 in place of the pipe organ. There were designs for new furnishings including a communion table, choir stalls, storage, lighting coronas for the north and south transepts and a new floor for the nave and aisles with underfloor heating.

To provide more community space, the architect proposed building two large parish rooms with fully accessible toilets, a kitchen and storage below the level of the churchyard on the north side of the church. This would utilise the one-storey drop in levels between the churchyard and road to give the new rooms an external wall with windows and an entrance. The rooms would be linked to the north aisle by a new stone stair with disabled access from road level. The undercroft, as it became known, received planning permission from SODC in June 1989.

The PCC submitted two petitions for faculties, for the undercroft in July 1989 and for the reordering in December 1990. Although the DAC did not oppose either petition, it raised concerns about some of the more radical aspects of the reordering to a Grade I listed medieval church. A couple of recent cases in the Diocese had caused controversy and it was felt that these proposals should be looked at in detail. The DAC also raised concerns about the serious implications for archaeological evidence involved in both sets of work. SODC had made it a condition

of planning approval that a complete archaeological assessment was to be undertaken on the relevant parts of the churchyard and church. In the response to the citation, letters had been received from two parishioners.

The Worshipful Chancellor of the Diocese, Mr Peter Boydell QC, recorded: 'In the light of the scale of the reordering, the significance of the proposal to construct the underground building and the implications for the archaeological evidence, I decided that both petitions should be considered at a sitting of the Consistory Court.'

The first hearing was on 14 March 1991, under the Chancellor. Evidence was heard from the Revd Chris Neal, who called nine witnesses including Robert Maguire, the churchwardens, the DAC and townspeople. Written evidence was submitted by the Oxford Archaeological Unit (OAU) and the Conservation Area Advisory Committee.

The PCC had undertaken a lot of research on previous changes to the church and its contents. It was able to show that the pulpit and the font were not in their original position and that a faculty had been issued in the nineteenth century to remove the pews, but never implemented. The PCC was also able to show when the building had last been lime-washed.

In his judgment, the Chancellor recorded that he was satisfied that both the proposals were pastorally necessary and acceptable, and that he was prepared to grant faculties on both petitions, subject to satisfactory resolution on three areas of disagreement between the PCC and the DAC. These were the positions of the pulpit and the north transept screen and agreement on the design of the junction between the stairs in the north-west corner of the church and the proposed undercroft. These were all resolved by July 1991.

The Chancellor stressed the need to take appropriate measures to deal with archaeological concerns. An assessment carried out by OAU in 1990 had determined that there were no substantial remains of earlier buildings in the area to the north and north-west of the church, but there were several medieval burials there which needed to be recorded and the remains reburied.

Although faculties had not been formally issued, the registrar gave oral consent to go ahead, but in September 1991 OAU reported that the works were damaging important medieval floor levels. The Chancellor ordered the works to be stopped and for two months lengthy discussions took place involving the PCC, the DAC, the architect, OAU and SODC.

The Chancellor decided that the hearing into both petitions should be resumed and a second hearing took place on 6 November 1991. The reordering petition was resolved when it was acknowledged that items of archaeological interest had been recorded and the architect proposed thinner floor slabs that would have less archaeological impact upon the subfloor of the nave. The plans were amended and a faculty issued. Resolution on the undercroft petition was reached when the Chancellor added a condition to the faculty requiring the PCC to undertake specific measures to protect archaeological deposits.

A Restoration Appeal Fund had been launched in 1989 under a newly formed Appeal Committee and about £300,000 was raised to pay for the reordering works. This came largely from the sale of All Saints, a late-nineteenth-century tin church, a legacy of £50,000 and direct giving by the congregation.

The reordering works went ahead and the building was reopened just before Christmas 1991. Part of the architect's vision was to improve the quality of light in the building. The church has virtually no stained glass, but even so it had been very gloomy, with a dark blue carpet up the centre aisle and dark-stained pine pews. The original organ had blocked a fourteenth-century screen and a view of the north transept's fifteenth-century window. Its removal brought light into the crossing and on to the new altar table.

All the new furnishings were of light wood. The pews were replaced by light ash traditional-style chairs, designed by Robert Maguire and made by Bates and Lambourne of Milton Common, Oxfordshire. A new lighting scheme was installed and the building was lime-washed throughout. It now feels spacious and airy and works as a unified space; there is a real sense of peace. The unchanged chancel has become a form of chapel and a space for reflection.

The Thame Barns Centre, July 2013. PHOTO BP

Below The 55+ monthly gathering listening to the speaker, September 2012. PHOTO PAUL CHAMBERLAIN

Bottom Doors to the kitchen and toilets, 2013. PHOTO BP

Looking from behind the nave altar towards the west end, July 2013. PHOTO BP

The changes have altered the way the congregation worships. The chairs are usually arranged in a semicircle in the nave, extending into the north and south aisles. This layout focuses attention on the nave table beneath the tower, now raised up by the dais. Other layouts are chosen for different services and events. Ian Adams, who arrived as curate post-reordering, remembers his first visit when he felt 'the very special atmosphere'. For more contemplative services, all the chairs can be moved out so that people can sit on cushions on the floor 'and then even a small group of people can feel at home in the space instead of being overwhelmed by rows of empty chairs'.

The church building is well used by different community groups, such as the University of the Third Age, and for concerts. There are regular lunches for senior citizens and mother and toddler groups, when tables are put out.

For the Revd Alan Garratt, who became Team

Rector in 2008, the key point is the flexibility. 'One of our values is that we want to be very family-friendly and family-shaped. A building that can only be used for set functions and everyone facing forward would not lend itself to that, so it has had a major effect.'

The undercroft plans were in the end abandoned. Further archaeological investigations revealed Saxon burials and there was growing local opposition to the removal of any burials. The reordering has enabled community activities to take place in the church itself.

The PCC was also developing Church Farm Barn, about 200yds from the church, which it had bought in a 50/50 partnership with the town council. Now the Thame Barns Centre, it is available for functions such as wedding receptions. The PCC has to rent space, but has first option on Sundays when it is used for church Sunday groups.

This scheme is now over twenty years old and, as the Revd Alan Garratt says, 'One of the downsides of being first on the block is that you see how some things would now be done differently.' The chairs don't stack, which means that it takes effort to move them, although the large congregation means there is no shortage of volunteers. In 2011, the toilets were adapted to become more accessible. The PCC is also facing up to the fact that the underfloor heating system needs attention and the lighting scheme should be revised.

CHALLENGES
The Consistory Court took up a huge amount of time and energy.

BEST PIECE OF ADVICE
It can be a positive step to have to leave your building for a while. We were out of the building for six months and a year might have been even better. It allows you to refresh how you do things and develop new ways.

WEBSITE
www.stmarysthame.org.uk

ST MARY LE MORE, WALLINGFORD

Once all the work was done, the congregation felt they wanted to leave the church open and it has been open daily for the last three years. It's just wonderful to see so many people coming in and being able to find a quiet space in the centre of a busy town. The Revd David Rice

Wallingford is a small, busy market town with a population of 7,500 in the Upper Thames Valley. The church is right in the centre of the market-place, near the town hall.

The Grade II* listed church existed by 1077, then as part of St Alban's Abbey. The west tower was originally twelfth-century, its upper stages rebuilt in about 1653. The church was rebuilt in 1854 to the design of the architect David Brandon working in the Gothic Revival style.

THE PROJECT

Between 2008 and 2010 a major restoration and reordering project was undertaken. Various rooms and enclosed spaces built forty or so years ago were removed and the tower was re-enclosed to provide storage and a vestry with a community meeting room above.

The pews and other items of unused furniture were removed and new seating and a dais were introduced. Underfloor heating was laid under a new floor and two toilets, one fully accessible, were installed at the west end of the north aisle. A kitchen and a café area were created in the south aisle.

The walls were restored and redecorated throughout and a new lighting scheme installed. The font was moved from the west end to the east end of the south aisle. Access for disabled people was improved at the north main entrance and a ramp to the dais was provided on the south side.

REALISATION

In the 1970s and 1980s separate spaces had been created for various activities. A previous incumbent, an architect, designed what was called the Gallery Room, a first-floor community room above the north aisle. Underneath, at the north entrance, a lobby was installed. The Gallery Room had a small kitchen and had been well used but in recent years its use had been restricted to no more than thirty people at a time, for safety reasons. The west tower had been glazed, with a vestry below and a Sunday School room above. Overall this area had what has been described as a rather 1970s 'Swiss Cottage' feel.

Before these works, the chancel end of the north aisle, known as the All Hallows Chapel, had been screened off and used for midweek communions. The chancel end of the south aisle had also been screened off and was used as a choir vestry.

Jeremy Bell of JBKS Architects was brought in to make sense of the building and found that 'this piecemeal closing-in of different parts of the building had so encroached on the architectural form that the overall integrity of the space had been almost completely compromised. Standing in the nave, we were in "the space left over". Coming in through the north entrance meant that when you entered the church you first came into a low-ceilinged lobby and then through another pair of doors into a "trough" between some pews; you could only really look around once you had got into the central aisle.'

The PCC was also looking at how to widen the church's engagement with the local community. The location right on the market square meant there was potential, but the very small site, on land mostly occupied by gravestones and some enormous beech trees, meant that there was no possibility of building any kind of hall or extension. It was clear that, to create a worship space that also allowed for increased community engagement, major changes to the interior would be needed.

Many discussions took place involving architects, congregation and PCC. It was agreed early on that the screen in the south aisle should be relocated, which would restore a view of the window at the east end of the aisle.

A key issue was a rather large mock-medieval rood screen with figures of the saints and the Virgin Mary, installed in 1925. Jeremy Bell had been given a late Victorian photograph showing the building before the rood screen and he proposed to the PCC that the screen should go, thereby restoring the long view down the nave to the chancel. The PCC had very mixed feelings, but agreement was reached to dismantle the screen as long as the main sculptures were kept.

However, the DAC, while positive about the idea of reopening the space, insisted that the rood screen be retained. They suggested that the lobby and the gallery room above it in the north aisle could be removed. Jeremy Bell explains that 'this was a really crucial moment. In its time very innovative, the room was still extremely useful to the church and was being used for a toddlers' group, so it was central to making contact with generations of young mothers and children.' It was also being used for regular coffee mornings.

Once it was decided to remove the internal rooms and screens, except for those in the tower, the PCC had to think again about how the church could be used. The opened-up space would have to become the hall as well as the church.

St Mary's is the first church in Oxfordshire to put a kitchen at the back of the church itself rather than enclose it in a room with a hatchway. Its position, at the west end of the south aisle, is discreet. The cooker, fridge and dishwasher all have cabinet lids which can be closed. In front is an elegant servery with black glass and a granite top. Visually the café area impresses visitors as a separate space, freed up by the removal of the pews to accommodate chairs and tables.

The tower space has been re-enclosed and two rooms retained. The upper Tower Room is reached by stairs just inside the north entrance. The lower room is the clergy vestry and can also be used for small meetings. Its double doors can be fully opened to allow extra seating for special occasions.

The PCC specifically chose Howe chairs, which are light and can be stacked forty high on trolleys in a very small space. This is essential when rapid change is needed from one activity to another.

The removal of the internal rooms, the repainted white walls, the introduction of a new pale tiled floor and pale wood chairs and the improved lighting have created a bright and spacious interior. You now enter this space straight from the street through a pair of glass doors.

Another key issue was how to integrate the chancel with the bright new nave and aisles. It was decided to paint the chancel walls a dark terracotta, chosen to match the red found in the marble reredos. The strong colour subdues the effect of the rather large and gloomy memorials. The rood screen ceases to dominate the space because it is no longer in such stark relief in front of a light chancel. The richness of the chancel and the colours of the rood screen work together and help to visually close off the chancel as a separate space, which is now used for quiet reflection.

The original estimate of building costs was £400,000, but because of inflation and additional, unforeseen works – the uncovering of a collapsed vault under the chancel, for instance – the final building costs were close to £410,000. However, the cost of chairs, fitted storage units in various areas, kitchen fittings and equipment, the new sound system and various smaller items brought the overall cost to just over £600,000, which was raised over four years of hard work. The PCC was able to contribute £200,000 from church reserves, which included the proceeds from the sale of a curate's house.

Grants came from SODC's Community Investment Fund (£100,000), Biffa (£50,000) and the Oxfordshire Historic Churches Trust. An appeal and local fund-raising produced £20,000; there was further support from the parish's Friends Group and from many individuals.

The PCC consulted the wider community

Top left Interior showing the pews, rood screen and white walls of the chancel before works done, January 2005. PHOTO JW

Top right Exterior from the south-west, March 2010.
PHOTO JOHN HURRELL, JBKS ARCHITECTS

Bottom Chairs set out for a service, March 2010.
PHOTO JOHN HURRELL, JBKS ARCHITECTS

via articles and a questionnaire in a monthly town magazine distributed to every house. The questionnaire asked how people would like the church to be used and developed, and elicited mainly positive feedback. Later on, another questionnaire was sent to all the Wallingford community organisations and clubs, specifically asking them how they would use the new building. There was a 58% response, which showed that footfall in the church would probably treble during an average week, in both daytime and evenings. About a dozen letters of endorsement were received from groups saying they would use the building. This was provided as evidence to support the PCC's successful application to the SODC Community Investment Fund.

Some of the groups that said they wanted to use the building have come along, while others, disappointingly, have not, such as an adult education group that lost its funding. Many diverse groups, however, have emerged to use the space in a wide range of ways and the building is now being used most mornings and evenings. The upper Tower Room offers a private meeting space for such events as the monthly meetings of the Cruse Bereavement and Friendship group. Space is cleared in the south aisle for mother and toddler groups so that they are close to the kitchen. Movable screens, which are also noticeboards, lock together and can be used to enclose the whole of the south aisle or to divide up any other area. The Baby Group meets upstairs in the Tower Room, which is also used for Children's Church on Sundays.

There are coffee mornings every Monday, Tuesday, Friday and Saturday to take advantage of the busiest market days. The Tuesday coffee morning is run by Style Acre, a local organisation for people with learning disabilities. There are regular concerts and numerous other groups hire the space in the evenings. It is really only underused in the afternoons and the PCC is working to identify additional potential users. It has an online booking form and an online calendar that shows what activities are taking place.

The previous interior had no longer worked well as worship space. The altar now sits on a raised dais, and the chairs are arranged so that everyone has a clear view of the services. The Revd David Rice says that 'people speak very movingly about the way that we worship now and there is a greater sense of belonging to each other. We have been experimenting with different styles of worship now that the chairs can be put out in different configurations to fit particular services and congregations.' There is a group working on developing and broadening the styles of worship, which could possibly include Café Church.

CHALLENGES

The PCC is trying to get the balance right between the overall cost of running the building and the income from lettings. Utilities costs have gone up through inflation and because the church is used so much more. The committee is currently researching letting charges at other Wallingford venues to ensure that when they do have to increase their charges, they do not under- or overcharge. Encouraging diverse community groups to use this unique space to its full potential is an ongoing process.

WEBSITE

http://www.marylemore.co.uk/

View of the west end showing the glazed-in tower with new storage cupboards in the lower room and the Tower Room above, July 2013. To the right are the toilets and stairs to the Tower Room. PHOTO BP

Above Looking towards the chancel, showing the rood screen installed in 1934, March 2010.
PHOTO JOHN HURRELL, JBKS ARCHITECTS

Right Singing Babies group in the Tower Room, 2013.
PHOTO MAVIS BOLTON

Below The servery at the west end of the south aisle, July 2013.
PHOTO BP

Below right The south aisle laid out for café mornings, July 2013.
PHOTO BP

St Mary the Virgin, Witney

Encouraging the maximum use of this ancient and beautiful church by restoring it to its full glory will benefit local people, have a transformative impact on cultural and community life and secure the future of the building. Catriona Robertson, Social Audit for St Mary the Virgin, January 2012

Witney is the largest town in West Oxfordshire, with a population of 27,000. The High Street Methodist Church has recently completed a major reordering including creating a café space. Witney is large enough to support both this and St Mary's, and there are plenty of surrounding satellite villages with no facilities. St Mary's stands at one end of Church Green, right at the edge of the busy town centre, and its tall spire makes it a landmark for miles around.

The Grade 1 listed church dates back to the eleventh century. The Norman church was incorporated as the nave into the present building, which was dedicated in 1243. In the fourteenth century a number of side chapels and some of the present windows were added. In the fifteenth century the south transept was extended and the present west nave window added. The building was restored and reordered between 1865 and 1869 by G. E. Street. It is of cruciform plan, with the tower over the crossing.

THE PROJECT

Phase 1, the comprehensive repair of the roofs of the north and south transepts, and the nave and associated stonework, so as to render the building watertight and weatherproof, was completed in December 2010. It cost £330,000.

Phase 2 is a major renewal and reordering of the interior which will involve the reflooring of the whole church; the installation of underfloor heating; a new lighting system; major refurnishing of the nave and the sanctuary area; the relocation of the Lady Chapel; the provision of further office space; and the extension of the kitchen and toilet facilities.

REALISATION

In the 1980s toilets were installed in the south porch and the multi-purpose Winchester Room was built in the south transept. A parish office and vestry were created in the Wenman Room at the west end of the north aisle because separate spaces were needed for different activities, including a soundproof area for children.

In 2008 an urgent need for major roof repairs was identified. The PCC also recognised that a major interior restoration and reordering would be necessary if the church were to continue to meet the needs of the community and its growing congregation. The floor, a mixture of tiles, concrete and wood, is in very poor condition, the heating inefficient and the interior shabby. The different areas seem unconnected and there is a wish to return to the sense of the building as one space, which can be used for different purposes. This is one reason for the desire to paint it white throughout.

Inside, it is light, spacious, and exceptionally wide for a church built to a cruciform plan. It is the largest medieval building in West Oxfordshire and has the largest capacity in the area, seating more than 600 people.

The PCC's vision is for the church to become what it calls 'The Venue', a multi-purpose building that will become a major cultural focus for the area. St Mary's is already used for important civic occasions, film festivals, exhibitions and a wide range of fund-raising and musical events, from Elvis Nights and acoustic evenings to a performance of Haydn's *Creation* with a full orchestra and choir. It is also used by some local schools for special occasions such as

Above Exterior from the north, July 2012. PHOTO JW

Right Interior before the pews were removed, May 2006. PHOTO JW

Below The Winchester Room in the south transept, July 2013. PHOTO BP

Year Seven introductory services, harvest and carol services, nativity plays and concerts. Its capacity to accommodate parents as well as staff and pupils is important and its acoustics and architecture give a sense of occasion to special events, which sports and drama halls struggle to provide.

The Revd Toby Wright, Team Rector, says, 'We feel a strong sense of call to the community and are completely committed to engage with it, serving it in a wide variety of ways. We want to be able to offer a sacred space, but also a space for building and strengthening community.'

In 2012, the church held its first beer festival and repeated the event in 2013. It sold out both years, even though in the second year there was twice as much beer as in the first. Mr Wright says it is 'an amazing opportunity to engage with people who have come from Witney and the surrounding areas and who otherwise would not have come into the building, and it offers some fantastic opportunities for pastoral engagement and support of the local community'. In 2013 it hosted Witney's first ever Food and Drink Festival, offering local food producers the chance to promote and sell their wares. This was again a success that the PCC intends to repeat.

In 2011 the PCC commissioned a social audit as part of its campaign appeal. The report, published in January 2012, recommended that St Mary's play to its main strengths: the richness and beauty it brings to performances and cultural events, the wide range of curriculum areas for which it can offer a teaching resource, and the quiet space it offers to those seeking a place for contemplation. The report stressed that in order for St Mary's to reach its full potential in all these areas, the seating, lighting, heating and catering facilities had to be improved. This was underlined by interviews with current users. The report recommended that it should collaborate with other professionals to develop its work in particular areas such as creating teacher resource packs for the different Key Stages in a range of subject areas. Another important idea is to offer improved presentation of some of the monuments and interpretation material for visitors.

The PCC is working with Jeremy Bell of JBKS Architects. The Revd Toby Wright explains that 'in the past people have tended to do separate pieces of work at different times without thinking of the whole. We need to work with the architect and the DAC to ensure that there is a coherent plan for the building and that we work with the history and architecture of the building and produce something of excellence.' The PCC is taking the advice of an archaeologist, a tile expert, a lighting expert and an expert in interior church refurbishment.

The plan is to extend the Winchester Room and add a second floor and gallery to provide additional meeting space. The PCC has been working with a local catering company to upgrade the kitchen facilities so that professional catering can be provided on-site for weddings, funerals, special church services and cultural events. Space can also be made available for corporate hire, which will help bring in an income to support the long-term maintenance of the building.

The south porch will be developed to provide upgraded and additional toilets, a spiral stair and a lift up to the Winchester Room's Upper Room. Thanks to the height of the Wenman Room, a second floor can be inserted to provide small meeting rooms and improved office space.

The liturgical space is also being developed. The intention is to open up the areas near the transepts, which will allow greater visibility from the seating there. As an interim measure, it is proposed to remove the dais on which the principal altar currently sits, in order to experience the flexibility of space on one level, and to move the altar further west. The intention is to commission new liturgical furniture from a local craftsman. The chancel will be developed as the centre of sacred space within the church. During the week the Daily Office will be prayed there, weekday Eucharists offered and visitors will be able to find a quiet place for reflection. Mr Wright explains that 'we also envisage this as the space where experimental worship, including our regular Taizé services, can be conducted. The improvements will enrich the worshipping life of the church, allowing for a range of liturgical expression to meet the needs of a growing and active town.'

A major challenge has been the long-drawn-out disagreement with the Victorian Society, which objected to the removal of the pews on the grounds that they were designed by the architect G. E. Street and were a significant element of the church's fixtures and fittings. They proposed that St Mary's was large enough to achieve its desired flexible space while retaining and relocating the pews. The Society took the PCC to a Consistory Court, only to withdraw a few days before the hearing, but not before the PCC had spent considerable time and money on a defence. Mr Wright comments that they 'were saddened the Victorian Society responded so strongly at the beginning when in fact no evidence was found to show that the pews were designed by G. E. Street'.

Once the Consistory Court was cancelled, the diocesan Chancellor awarded a faculty and the pews were removed at the end of 2012. Ten pews have been relocated in various places around the church. The rest have been replaced by 160 Howe 40/4 chairs. This has met one of the church's key priorities, says Mr Wright, 'which is to use the building as flexibly as possible, and being able to stack 160 chairs in less than 1.85 metres of space is of huge importance to us'.

The current estimate for the total cost of the project is £2 million. Fund-raising started in August 2008. Applications for grants were submitted to a number of Trust Funds and English Heritage, and this raised £235,400. A direct appeal to those on the Electoral Roll brought in a further £10,000. By January 2013, about £370,000 had been raised, most of which has been spent on the roof work.

The restoration and renewal phase, which is expected to cost £1.7 million, was launched at a reception in March 2011 in the presence of HRH The Princess Royal.

The PCC is aware that finding the money is going to be a major challenge, especially in a recession. Its members are optimistic, however. Mr Wright says, 'There are an increasing number of people who are approaching us wanting to do concerts, art festivals, musical festivals and film festivals in the building.'

CHALLENGE

Ideally, the PCC would have liked to raise the entire sum before starting work, but, realising that this could take years, it has decided to break the project down into small affordable stages, which can be undertaken as soon as the money is to hand. 'This will enable us to keep moving gradually and keep up momentum,' says Mr Wright, 'and people are more likely to invest if they can see that things are happening.'

WEBSITE
http://witneyparish.org.uk/

Top Looking towards the east end showing the new chairs, July 2013. PHOTO BP

Bottom The Witney Food Festival taking place in the church, May 2013. PHOTO ROSEMARY HARRIS

ACKNOWLEDGEMENTS

For their unstinting help with individual case studies the author is immensely grateful to: Revd Mark Abrey, Revd John Acreman, Dr Garry Alder, Gillian Argyle, John Beaumont, Jeremy Bell, David Birkett, Revd Richard Bittleston, Revd Mark Blamey, Mavis Bolton, Revd Kat Bracewell, Carolyn Brown, Ian Brown, Revd Janice Chilton, Michael Clews, Revd Canon Ian Cohen, Revd Richard Coombs, Revd Kevin Davies, Anna Dulnikowska-Przystalska, Revd Maggie Durran, Helena Fickling, Revd Jan Fielden, Camilla Finlay, David Finlay, Jim Flux, Margaret Forey, Matt Freer, Revd Canon Judy French, David Gambier, Revd Alan Garratt, Revd Jeremy Goulston, David Greasby, Bob Gregory, Canon Richard Hancock, Revd Christobel Hargraves, Janette Hathaway, Dorothy Howarth, Samantha Hughes, Revd Caroline King, Elizabeth MacLeod, Natalie Merry, Revd Dr Charles Miller, Revd Canon Chris Neal, Mike Peckett, Rosemary Perrow, Diana Pettifer, Revd Tony Price, Margaret Pritchard, Sylvia Reddington, Revd David Rice, David Rogers, Alison Shaw, Revd Jane Sherwood, Andrew Smith, Daphne Stallwood, Ann Stead, Mike Summers, Neil Sutherland, Olive Sutcliffe, James Taylor, Stephen Thomas, Revd Dr Hugh White, the Very Revd Robert Wilkes, Gill Withers, Revd Toby Wright, John Wyatt.

In addition, the Oxfordshire Historic Churches Trust must express deep gratitude to the following individuals and organisations who kindly contributed funds for this project: Allchurches Trust; David Barnett; The J. Paul Getty Jnr Charitable Trust; St Michael's and All Saints Charities; The Bishop of Oxford's Outreach Fund; The Sandford Trust, and other generous supporters of the project who prefer to remain anonymous.

OHCT and the author are also grateful to the photographers whose names appear in the captions and who own the copyright in their photographs. JW is John Ward and BP is Becky Payne.

Special thanks must go to John Ward, who not only gave us access to his existing collection of photographs of Oxfordshire churches, but also enthusiastically volunteered to travel around the county to photograph many of these projects. All his photographs can be seen at http://www.flickr.com/photos/oxfordshirechurches/collections/72157600269843044.

The map of Oxfordshire is derived from a basemap by Nilfanion, created using Ordnance Survey data. It is licensed under the Creative Commons Attribution-Share Alike 3.0 Unported licence and contains Ordnance Survey data © Crown copyright and database rights.

For his continuing support and his unerring belief that it was going to happen, this project owes a debt of gratitude to the Rt Revd Colin Fletcher, Bishop of Dorchester. It was his idea and it was his leadership that kept it moving forward to a successful fruition.

Huge thanks, too, to the Oxfordshire Historic Churches Trust (OHCT) and to Charles Baker, its former Chairman, and Basil Eastwood, the current Chairman. Not only was OHCT partly responsible for initiating the project but it also provided support throughout the project's development with advice and specialised knowledge of all the churches in the county.

Grateful thanks to Simon Haviland for giving the project the benefit of his invaluable knowledge of publishing and ensuring we understood the practical detail that has to go into the production of a book. He kept us all on track and gently reminded us when a deadline was approaching. Key to the success was Elisabeth Ingles who, as editor, sensitively and firmly ensured the overall consistency of the text and the elimination of mistakes and overwriting. Robert Carter is responsible for the design of the book and it is down to him that it is so easy to read and so attractively laid out.

Finally, thanks to my partner, Susan Miller, for patiently transcribing the telephone interviews and for her continual support, but especially for driving me around Oxfordshire for four days in July, visiting far too many churches than is normal for most people, and enjoying it.

Sources of Help and Guidance

ON LOOKING AFTER A CHURCH BUILDING AND DEVELOPING IT FOR WIDER COMMUNITY USE

The first place to go is to your denomination website.

The Churchcare website is maintained by the Church of England's Cathedral and Church Buildings Division, but is a comprehensive resource for anyone who has responsibility for a church building: http://www.churchcare.co.uk/

Most Church of England dioceses have very useful guidance on their own websites.

The Catholic Church in England and Wales: http://www.cbcew.org.uk/CBCEW-Home/Departments/Christian-Life-and-Worship/Patrimony

The Methodist Church: http://www.methodist.org.uk/ministers-and-office-holders/property

The Baptist Union of Great Britain: http://www.baptist.org.uk/Groups/220716/BUC_Legal_Property.aspx

The United Reformed Church: http://www.urc.org.uk/resources/plato-property-handbook.html

The Quakers: http://www.quaker.org.uk/property-matters

GENERAL GUIDANCE

The National Churches Trust offers a comprehensive resource centre covering all aspects of looking after and developing a place of worship. They also offer grants: http://www.nationalchurchestrust.org/

The County Churches Trusts are able to offer support and grants to places of worship of all denominations. To find details of your local Trust go to the National Churches Trust website (above).

The Arthur Rank Centre has compiled a comprehensive online resource: http://www.arthurrankcentre.org.uk/publications-and-resources/rural-church-buildings
The Churches Conservation Trust provides examples of

community-based extended uses helping sustain churches: http://www.visitchurches.org.uk/AboutCCT/Regeneratingcommunities/

The Churches Trust for Cumbria: http://www.ctfc.org.uk/

GUIDANCE ON HERITAGE

English Heritage is part of the regulatory process and also offers advice and support. In 2012 they published a revised edition of their guidance on New Work in Historic Places of Worship: http://www.english-heritage.org.uk/caring/places-of-worship/

The Heritage Lottery Fund provides a range of good-practice guidance: http://www.hlf.org.uk/HowToApply/goodpractice/Pages/Goodpracticeguidance.aspx#.Ukmiv4akrSI

You may well have to consult one or more of the Amenity Societies. They are also a good source of advice.

The Ancient Monuments Society: http://www.ancientmonumentssociety.org.uk/

The Society for the Protection of Ancient Buildings: www.spab.org.uk

The Georgian Group: www.georgiangroup.org.uk

The Victorian Society: www.victoriansociety.org.uk

The Twentieth Century Society: www.c20society.org.uk

GUIDANCE ON COMMUNITY PROJECTS

The Diocese of Hereford (Church of England) has produced a toolkit, *Crossing the Threshold: a community development approach to the use of church buildings*, a step-by-step guide to developing and delivering sustainable community projects in church buildings. The latest version can be downloaded here: http://www.hereford.anglican.org/churchgoers/community_partnership_and_funding/about_us_and_latest_news/index.aspx

Resourcing Christian Community Action brings together current best practice in Christian care in local communities with a resources and knowledge base: http://www.how2help.net/
Approach your local authority (ask for Community Development)

or local strategic partnership (your local authority can point you in their direction).

Your local voluntary and community sector (VCS) infrastructure organisation can provide vital support for voluntary organisations and community groups: http://www.navca.org.uk/directory

Community Tool Box covers all aspects of setting up community projects: http://ctb.ku.edu/en/

The Village SOS website offers tools, support and expert guidance to help communities start their own community businesses/social enterprises: http://www.villagesos.org.uk/

The 38 Community Councils are charitable local development agencies that make up the Rural Community Action Network (RCAN) and can offer advice, support, and access to grant databases. To find your Community Council visit www.acre.org.uk/

The Big Lottery website has a list of organisations that can provide advice: http://www.biglotteryfund.org.uk/funding/funding-guidance/applying-for-funding/external-help-and-advice

The Church Community Value toolkit helps churches calculate their financial contribution to the community and demonstrate their distinctiveness. Useful evidence to support grant applications. http://www.cuf.org.uk/act/resources-projects/community-value-toolkit

The Faith Based Regeneration Network UK (FBRN) is the leading national multi-faith network for community development, regeneration and social action: http://www.fbrn.org.uk/resources

GUIDANCE ON FUNDING

The Church of England's Parish Resources offers a range of funding guides to help you target funding for projects: http://www.parishresources.org.uk/resources-for-treasurers/funding/

The Big Lottery: http://www.biglotteryfund.org.uk/funding/funding-guidance/applying-for-funding

How to obtain funding from the Landfill Communities Fund: http://www.entrust.org.uk/home/lcf/about

MAJOR FUNDING SOURCES

The Heritage Lottery Fund: http://www.hlf.org.uk/

The Big Lottery: http://www.biglotteryfund.org.uk/

The Allchurches Trust: http://www.allchurches.co.uk/

The Church and Community Fund: http://www.ccfund.org.uk/

The National Churches Trust: http://www.nationalchurchestrust.org/

FUNDING DIRECTORIES

Heritage Alliance: http://www.theheritagealliance.org.uk/fundingdirectory/

The Architectural Heritage Fund: http://www.ahfund.org.uk/

Funding Central provides information on local and national sources of funding for charities and projects as well as training opportunities. You can subscribe to a free alert service to tell you about any new funding programmes that match your criteria: http://www.fundingcentral.org.uk/

The Directory of Social Change is the most comprehensive directory available: www.dsc.org.uk, www.trustfunding.org.uk and www.governmentfunding.org.uk. There is a registration fee, but your local authority or local library may be able to provide cheaper access.